Make-Ahead Menus

Great Meals in Minutes was created by Rebus Inc., and published by Time-Life Books.

This edition published 1994 by Bloomsbury Books, an imprint of The Godfrey Cave Group, 42 Bloomsbury Street, London, WC1B 3QJ.

© 1994 Time-Life Books BV.

ISBN 1 85471 591 7

Printed and bound in Great Britain.

Make-Ahead Menus

Jenifer Harvey Lang

Menu 1

Brigand's Brochettes	8
Baked Brussels Sprouts	
Radish Salad	

Menu 2

Fish Schnitzel	10
Steamed Parslied Potatoes	
Red and Green Cabbage Salad	

Menu 3

| Baked Fish with Pecan Stuffing | 13 |
| Cauliflower, Bell Pepper, and Olive Salad | |

Marilyn Hansen

Menu 1

| Beef Stroganoff with Kasha | 18 |
| Beetroot and Oranges Vinaigrette | |

Menu 2

| Bouillabaisse with Croutons and Rouille | 20 |
| Tomato-Chutney Aspic | |

Menu 3

| Swedish Meatballs | 23 |
| Cucumber and Radish Salad | |

Margaret Fraser

Menu 1

Taramosalata with Crudités and Pitta Bread	28
Lamb Kebabs	
Stuffed Tomatoes	

Menu 2

Chilled Avgolemono	31
Spanakopita	
Marinated Artichokes with Greek Olives	

Menu 3

Moussaka	35
Lettuce with Cucumber-Yogurt Dressing	
Sesame Pitta Crisps/Melon with Ouzo Cream	

Roberta Rall

Menu 1

| Spinach and Potato Soup | 40 |
| Salmon and Pasta Sunburst Salad with Herbed Mustard Sauce | |

Menu 2

Seafood Provençal in Parchment	42
Lacy Potato Pancakes	
Honeydew-Avocado Salad	

Menu 3

Raclette Casseroles	46
Marinated Vegetable Salad	
Fruit in Filo Bundles	

Gloria Zimmerman

Menu 1

Thai Seafood Salad	52
Ginger Chicken	
White Rice	

Menu 2

| Vietnamese Salad | 54 |
| Poached Chicken with Rice and Ginger Sauce | |

Menu 3

Sour Beef Salad	58
Sweet Pork	
Broccoli with Oyster Sauce	

Bloomsbury Books
London

Jenifer Harvey Lang

Menu 1
(right)
Brigand's Brochettes
Baked Brussels Sprouts
Radish Salad

Jenifer Lang says that over the years she has come to prefer 'down-to-earth cooking that leaves guests full and immensely satisfied.' After marrying restaurateur George Lang and travelling with him to his native Hungary, she discovered that the cuisine of that country particularly suited her taste. All three of her menus typify meals you might eat in Middle European homes, and all can be prepared the day before or the day of serving. The main dishes go directly from the refrigerator into the broiler, oven, or frying pan.

Menu 1 features brigand's brochettes, reputedly created long ago by Hungarian robbers who never stayed in one place long enough to cook anything more complex than grilled meats and vegetables. If you wish, serve the brochettes in traditional Hungarian style by balancing the skewers atop thick slices of deep-fried bread. Baked Brussels sprouts with sour cream and radish salad are the accompaniments.

Schnitzel made with ground fish is the focus of Menu 2. The fish is shaped into patties, coated with egg and bread crumbs, and then refrigerated. Just before serving, the patties are fried to a golden brown and topped with a tangy horseradish sauce. Steamed parslied potatoes and cabbage salad are traditional partners for the *schnitzel.*

Menu 3 is a dramatic meal that provides each person with a whole baked fish stuffed with a nut and breadcrumb filling. Marinated cauliflower and bell pepper salad makes a light and refreshing counterpoint to the fish.

Note: In all these recipes, tablespoon measurements are level tablespoons unless otherwise specified.

Simple flowers and dinnerware suit this easy Hungarian meal of skewered vegetables and meat, radish salad, and baked Brussels sprouts topped with sour cream.

Brigand's Brochettes
Baked Brussels Sprouts
Radish Salad

The baked Brussels sprouts casserole is very simple to assemble and would be equally good made with cauliflower, turnips, or new potatoes – or a mixture of these vegetables. Brussels sprouts resemble tiny cabbages and have a delicate cabbage flavour. Buy compact, bright green sprouts; avoid any that are wilted or yellowing.

For the brochettes, select vegetables of roughly uniform size. The new potatoes, onions, and mushroom caps should be about 3½ cm (1½ inches) in diameter.

What to drink
A full-bodied white wine, such as a good-quality California Chardonnay, would be fine here. For authenticity, serve the Hungarian Egri Bikavér.

Start-to-Finish Steps

The day before or the morning of serving
1   Follow brochettes recipe steps 1 through 5.
2   While potatoes are cooling, follow Brussels sprouts recipe steps 1 through 3.
3   While Brussels sprouts are cooking, follow brochettes recipe steps 6 and 7.
4   Follow Brussels sprouts recipe steps 4 and 5, and brochettes recipe steps 8 and 9 if desired.
5   Follow salad recipe steps 1 and 2.

Thirty minutes before serving
1   Follow Brussels sprouts recipe step 6 and salad recipe step 3.
2   Follow brochettes recipe step 10.
3   While brochettes are grilling, follow salad recipe step 4.
4   Follow brochettes recipe steps 11 and Brussels sprouts recipe step 7. (If using combination oven-broiler, place casserole on lower rack.)
5   While brochettes and Brussels sprouts are cooking, follow salad recipe step 5.
6   Follow brochettes recipe step 12, Brussels sprouts recipe step 8, and serve with salad.

Brigand's Brochettes

6 or 7 small new potatoes (about 350 g (12 oz) total weight)
850 g (1¾ lb) hot Italian link sausage
250 g (8 oz) slab bacon, sliced 1 cm (½ inch) thick (about 3 slices)
5 small onions (about 750 g (1½ lb) total weight)
3 medium-size red bell peppers (about 500 g (1 lb) total weight)
16 medium-size mushrooms (about 500 g (1 lb) total weight)
Salt and freshly ground pepper
250 ml (8 fl oz) olive oil
2½ ltrs (4 pts) vegetables oil (optional)
1 loaf unsliced firm-textured brown or white bread (optional)

1   Bring 1¼ ltrs (2 pts) water to a boil in large saucepan over high heat.
2   Meanwhile, scrub potatoes. Cut sausage crosswise into 1½ cm (¾ inch) pieces. Cut bacon into 2½ cm (1 inch) pieces. Set aside.
3   Add potatoes to boiling water and cook over medium heat 15 minutes, or until almost cooked through.
4   Meanwhile, peel onions and cut into 5 mm (¼ inch) slices. Wash bell peppers and dry with paper towels. Halve, core, and seed peppers, and cut into 2½ cm (1 inch) squares. Wipe mushrooms clean with damp paper towels. Remove stems and reserve for another use. Set mushroom caps aside.
5   Turn potatoes into colander to drain and cool slightly.
6   Cut potatoes into 1 cm (½ inch) slices. Thread eight 30 cm (12 inch) skewers as follows: Start with mushroom cap and alternate pieces of potato, sausage, bell pepper, bacon, and onion in any order you like. (Leave about 5 cm (2 inches) of skewer free if using bread.) Finish each skewer with a mushroom cap. Season brochettes with salt and pepper.
7   Place brochettes in jelly-roll pan or on large platter, in 2 layers if necessary. Pour olive oil over brochettes and turn each to coat with oil. Cover pan with plastic wrap and refrigerate until 20 minutes before serving.
8   If using bread, heat 2½ ltrs (4 pts) vegetable oil in

large, deep heavy-gauge skillet until temperature of oil registers 180°–200°C (350°F–400°F) on deep-fat thermometer. (You should keep temperature within this range while frying.)

9 Meanwhile, line large plate with double thickness of paper towels. Trim bread loaf to measure 20 x 7¹/₂ x 7¹/₂ cm (8 x 3 x 3 inches); cut loaf into eight 2¹/₂ cm (1 inch) slices. Cut shallow notch in one side of each sice. Working in batches if necessary, deep fry bread in hot oil, turning once, about 2 minutes, or until crisp. Using tongs, transfer fried bread to paper-towel-lined plate and when cool cover loosely with plastic wrap until needed.

10 Twenty minutes before serving, preheat broiler. Turn brochettes to coat with olive oil and arrange on rack in broiler pan. Broil 10 cm (4 inches) from heat 10 minutes. Reserve olive oil for basting.

11 Turn brochettes, baste with reserved olive oil, and broil another 10 minutes, or until meat and vegetables are browned.

12 To serve, place 2 fried bread slices, if using, notched side up, on opposite sides of 4 dinner plates. Balance a skewer between each pair of bread slices. Spoon pan juices ove bread and brochettes and serve. Place remaining brochettes on platter, cover with aluminium foil, and keep warm on stovetop.

Baked Brussels Sprouts

1 Kg (2 lb) Brussels sprouts (about 24 medium-size sprouts)
2¹/₂ tablespoons unsalted butter
Salt
Freshly ground pepper
175 g (6 oz) sour cream
45 g (1¹/₂ oz) unseasoned dry bread crumbs

1 In large saucepan fitted with vegetable steamer, bring about 2¹/₂ cm (1 inch) water to a boil over high heat.

2 Meanwhile, wash and trim Brussels sprouts.

3 Place sprouts in steamer, cover pan, and cook 10 minutes.

4 Drain sprouts and turn into medium-size ovenproof casserole.

5 Melt butter in small saucepan over medium heat. Pour butter over sprouts and season with salt and pepper to taste. Cover casserole with plastic wrap and refrigerate until 30 minutes before serving.

6 Thirty minutes before serving, uncover casserole and set out to come to room temperature.

7 Ten minutes before serving, spoon sour cream

evenly over sprouts and sprinkle with bread crumbs. Bake sprouts in very hot oven until heated through.

8 Serve sprouts directly from casserole or spoon sprouts and topping carefully onto serving platter.

Radish Salad

750 g (1¹/₂ lb) red radishes
Small bunch chives
Small head curly leaf lettuce
Large lemon
4 tablespoons olive oil
Salt
Freshly ground pepper

1 Wash and dry radishes and chives. Trim radishes. Wrap radishes and chives tightly in plastic wrap and refrigerate until needed. Wash lettuce and dry with paper towels. Discard any bruised or discoloured leaves. Wrap lettuce in paper towels, enclose in plastic bag, and refrigerate until needed.

2 Halve lemon and squeeze enough juice to measure 3 tablespoons. Combine lemon juice, olive oil, and salt and pepper to taste in small jar with tight-fitting lid and shake until combined. Refrigerate dressing until 30 minutes before serving.

3 Thirty minutes before serving, set out dressing to come to room temperature.

4 In food processor fitted with slicing disc, or with paring knife, cut radishes into thin slices. Cut chives into 1 cm (¹/₂ inch) pieces. Combine radishes and chives in medium-size bowl. Shake dressing to recombine and pour over salad; toss to coat well.

5 To serve, divide lettuce leaves among 4 dinner plates and top with salad.

<table>
<tr>
<td>

Menu

2

</td>
<td>

Fish Schnitzel
Steamed Parslied Potatoes
Red and Green Cabbage Salad

</td>
</tr>
</table>

An extremely versatile main dish, the fish Schnitzel (which resemble croquettes) can be made with almost any variety of fresh fish. The patties benefit from standing in the refrigerator: The chilling time sets the breading and helps it adhere to the fish.

What to drink

An ideal wine with this meal would be a lightly chilled dry aromatic Gewürztraminer of medium body. Try one from Alsace, California, or the Pacific Northwest.

Start-to-Finish Steps

The day before or the morning of serving
1. Follow schnitzel recipe steps 1 through 8.
2. Follow potatoes recipe step 1.
3. Follow salad recipe steps 1 through 5.

Twenty minutes before serving
1. Follow potatoes recipe steps 2 and 3.
2. While potatoes are cooking, follow schnitzel recipe steps 9 and 10.
3. Follow salad recipe step 6, schnitzel recipe step 11, potatoes recipe step 4, and serve.

Fried fish patties topped with horseradish sauce are delicious with red and green cabbage salad and steamed potatoes sprinkled with chopped parsley.

Fish Schnitzel

2 slices firm home-style white bread
125 ml (4 fl oz) milk
6 eggs
Small onion
5 tablespoons unsalted butter
750 g (1½ lb) white-fleshed fish fillets, such as
    flounder, cod, haddock, or whiting
Salt and freshly ground pepper
125 g (4 oz) plain flour
100 g (3 oz) unseasoned dry bread crumbs
125 ml (4 fl oz) sour cream
1½ tablespoons prepared horseradish with beetroot
250 ml (8 fl oz) vegetable oil
Large lemon

1   Place bread in small bowl and pour in milk. Set bread aside to soak 5 minutes.

2   Meanwhile, separate 3 eggs, placing yolks in shallow bowl and reserving whites for another use. Peel onion and finely chop enough to measure 60 g (2 oz); set aside.

3   Drain off milk and squeeze bread almost dry; set aside.

4   Melt 2 tablespoons butter in small skillet over medium heat. Add onion and sauté, stirring occasionally, about 4 minutes, or until just translucent.

5   Wipe fish fillets with damp paper towels. Cut fillets into large pieces and place in food processor or blender. Add bread, egg yolks, and onion, and season with salt and pepper. Process, a few seconds at a time, until mixture is coarsely chopped and thoroughly blended. Do not purée.

6   Break remaining 3 eggs into shallow bowl and beat with fork. Place flour and bread crumbs in separate shallow bowls.

7   Divide fish mixture into 8 equal portions. Shape each portion into an oval patty about 1½ cm (¾ inch) thick. One at a time, coat patties with flour. Pat gently to remove excess. Dip patties into

beaten eggs to coat completely, then coat with bread crumbs. Place each breaded schnitzel on wire rack set on baking sheet. Cover pan and refrigerate.

8   In small bowl, stir together sour cream and horseradish. Cover and refrigerate.

9   Ten minutes before serving, heat remining 3 tablespoons butter with oil in 1 large or 2 medium-size heavy-gauge skillets over medium-high heat. When fat is hot but not smoking, add schnitzels in single layer and fry about 8 minutes, turning once. Reduce heat, if necessary, so they do not brown too quickly.

10 Meanwhile, wash and dry lemon and cut one half into 4 wedges. Reserve remainder.

11 Divide schnitzels among 4 dinner plates and top each serving with horseradish sauce and a lemon wedge.

Steamed Parslied Potatoes

750 g (1¹/₂ lb) new potatoes
Small bunch parsley
Salt

1   Peel potatoes; halve or quarter, depending on size. Place potatoes in large bowl of cold water; cover and refrigerate until needed.

2   Twenty minutes before serving, in large saucepan fitted with vegetable steamer, bring about 2¹/₂ cm (1 inch) water to a boil over high heat. Drain potatoes, place in steamer, and cook, covered, 15 minutes, or until tender.

3   Meanwhile, wash and dry parsley. Trim ends and discard. Finely chop 15 g (¹/₂ oz) parsley.

4   Divide potatoes among 4 dinner plates, or place in serving bowl, and sprinkle with parsley and salt.

Red and Green Cabbage Salad

Small head red cabbage (about 500 g (1 lb))
Small head green cabbage (about 500 g (1 lb))
1 or 2 scallions
125 ml (4 fl oz) red wine vinegar
1 tablespoon sugar
1 teaspoon salt
1 teaspoon caraway seeds

1   Bring 2 ltrs (3 pts) water to a boil in large saucepan over high heat.

2   Meanwhile, halve and core cabbages. Thinly slice enough red and green cabage to measure 500 g (1 lb).

3   Drop sliced cabbage into boiling water and blanch 1 minute. Turn cabbage into colander to drain.

4   Meanwhile, trim scallions and coarsely chop enough to measure 1 tablespoon. In food processor or blender, combine scallions, vinegar, sugar, and salt. Process about 20 seconds, or until ingredients are thoroughly mixed.

5   Transfer cabbage to large non-aluminium bowl. Pour dressing over cabbage, sprinkle with caraway seeds, and toss to combine. Cover bowl with plastic wrap and refrigerate until just before serving stirring 3 or 4 times.

6   To serve, toss cabbage and divide among 4 plates.

Baked Fish with Pecan Stuffing
Cauliflower, Bell Pepper, and Olive Salad

Whole baked stuffed fish with a salad of cauliflower, bell peppers, and olives is an impressive meal for company.

In Hungary, a cook preparing the fish recipe would use the firm-fleshed white fish called fogas, or its smaller relative, süllo, which taste like a cross between pike and perch. Since fogas and süllo are not available in this country, try pike, perch, trout, sea bass, or whiting.

What to drink

The cook suggests a red or white wine spritzer (wine mixed with club soda) as both an aperitif and an accompaniment to the meal. A simple dry white wine, such as a Soave or Orvieto from Italy, or a dry Chenin Blanc from California, would be a good match for these dishes.

Start-to-Finish Steps

The day before serving

1 Wash and dry parsley. Set aside 4 sprigs for garnish and chop enough remaining parsley to measure 3 tablespoons for fish recipe and 1 tablespoon for salad recipe.
2 Follow fish recipe steps 1 through 6.
3 Follow salad recipe steps 1 through 8.

Thirty minutes before serving

1 Follow fish recipe step 7 and salad recipe step 9.
2 Follow fish recipe step 8.
3 While fish is baking, follow salad recipe steps 10 and 11.
4 Follow fish recipe step 9 and serve with salad.

Baked Fish with Pecan Stuffing

10 slices firm home-style white bread
500 ml (1 pt) milk
2 eggs
60 g (2 oz) whole pecans or walnuts
3 tablespoons chopped parsley, plus 4 sprigs for garnish
Salt
Freshly ground pepper
4 whole firm-fleshed fish (about 350 g (12 oz) each), cleaned and boned, with heads and tails intact
4 tablespoons good-quality olive oil
2 tablespoons unsalted butter, well chilled
1 red radish for garnish (optional)

1 Place bread in medium-size bowl and pour in milk. Let bread soak 5 minutes.
2 Meanwhile, separate eggs, dropping yolks into container of food processor or blender and reserving whites for another use.
3 Drain bread and squeeze almost dry.
4 For stuffing, add bread, pecans or walnuts, chopped parsley, and salt and pepper to taste to egg yolks in food processor or blender. Process, turning machine on and off, no more than 15 seconds; nuts should not be too finely ground.

5 Rinse fish and pat dry with paper towels. Fill cavity of each fish with about 60 g (2 oz) stuffing; do not overfill, as stuffing will expand during baking. (Wrap any extra stuffing in foil to bake along with fish.) As each fish is stuffed, place in jelly-roll pan. Pour 1 tablespoon olive oil over each fish; using your hands, rub oil over skin of each fish to coat completely. Cover pan with plastic wrap and refrigerate until 30 minutes before serving.
6 Cut butter into 5 mm (1/4 inch) squares; wrap and refrigerate until 30 minutes before serving.
7 Thirty minutes before serving, preheat oven to 200°C (400°F or Mark 6). Wash and trim radish, if using, and cut into thin slices. Halve slices and set aside.
8 Season fish with salt and pepper and top each fish with a few squares of butter. Bake about 25 minutes, basting twice with pan juices, until outer flesh springs back readily when pressed with fingers and inner flesh appears opaque at fleshiest part when fish is pierced with a sharp knife.
9 Using wide metal spatula, transfer a fish to each of 4 dinner plates. Spoon some pan juices over each, and cover each fish eye with a parsley sprig, and some radish slices, if desired.

Cauliflower, Bell Pepper, and Olive Salad

Large head cauliflower (about 1 Kg (2 lb))
Small red bell pepper
Small green bell pepper
Small yellow bell pepper
10 extra-large pitted black olives
125 ml (4 fl oz) good-quality olive oil
1 tablespoon chopped parsley
1 tablespoon red or white wine vinegar
2 teaspoons Dijon mustard
2 flat anchovy fillets, or 2 teaspoons anchovy paste
Salt and freshly ground pepper
Large head lettuce

1 In large saucepan fitted with vegetable steamer, bring $2^1/_2$ cm (1 inch) water to a boil over high heat.
2 Meanwhile, wash and trim cauliflower and cut into florets. Place florets in steamer, cover pan, and cook 5 minutes.
3 While cauliflower cooks, wash and dry bell peppers. Halve, core, and seed peppers and cut lengthwise into thin strips; set aside.
4 Lift out steamer, reserving hot water in pan, and turn cauliflower into colander. Refresh under cold running water and set aside to drain.
5 Return water in pan to a boil. Replace steamer and add peppers. Cover pan and cook 1 minute. Meanwhile, drain olives and quarter lengthwise; place in large non-aluminium bowl.
6 Lift out steamer and turn peppers into large strainer; refresh peppers under cold running water and set aside to drain.
7 Meanwhile, for dressing combine olive oil, chopped parsley, vinegar, mustard, anchovies or anchovy paste, and salt and pepper to taste in blender. Blend about 15 seconds, or until emulsified.
8 Add cauliflower and peppers to olives in large non-aluminium bowl. Pour dressing over salad and toss well. Cover bowl with plastic wrap and refrigerate until 30 minutes before serving.
9 Thirty minutes before serving, remove salad from refrigerator. Toss salad and set aside to come to room temperature.
10 Wash lettuce and dry in salad spinner or with paper towels. Discard any bruised or discoloured leaves.
11 Place 2 or 3 large lettuce leaves on each dinner plate and top with salad.

Added touch
Hungary is famed for its pastries, and all Hungarian cooks have their own versions of this rich cottage cheese cake, known as *turós pite*. Meringue is piped on top in an appealing lattice pattern. Be sure to wash and dry the beaters and bowl after mixing the pastry dough; any trace of grease or egg yolk will keep the egg whites from beating up properly.

Latticed Cottage Cheese Cake

Pastry:
175 g (6 oz) plain flour
$1/_2$ teaspoon baking soda
Pinch of salt
4 tablespoons unsalted butter, at room temperature
60 ml (2 fl oz) sour cream
60 g (2 oz) sugar
1 egg, at room temperature

Topping:
175 g (6 oz) cottage cheese
4 tablespoons sour cream
125 g (4 oz) plus 2 tablespoons sugar
1 egg yolk, at room temperature
1 tablespoon plain flour
1 teaspoon finely grated orange zest
30 g (1 oz) golden raisins
2 egg whites, at room temperature

1 Preheat oven to 190°C (375°F or Mark 5).
2 Prepare pastry: In large bowl, combine flour, baking soda, salt, butter, and sour cream. Beat with electric mixer about 1 minute, or until mixture resembles coarse cornmeal. Add sugar and egg and mix about 15 seconds, or just until dough forms a ball. Press dough into $22^1/_2$ cm (9 inch) square cake pan.
3 Bake pastry 20 minutes. Wash and dry beaters and bowl.
4 While pastry bakes, prepare topping: In food processor, combine cottage cheese, sour cream, 60 g (2 oz) sugar, the egg yolk, and orange zest. Process about 15 seconds, or until puréed. With rubber spatula, fold in raisins.
5 Place egg whites in large bowl and beat with electric mixer until frothy. Add remaining sugar and continue beating until soft peaks form.
6 After cake has baked 20 minutes, remove pan from oven and pour cottage cheese topping over cake. Fill pastry bag fitted with medium-size round tip with beaten egg whites and pipe meringue over topping in lattice pattern, making 4 strips in each direction. Or, spoon meringue onto topping in lattice patern.
7 Return cake to oven and bake an additional 15 minutes, or until topping is firm and meringue is browned. Let cake cool to room temperature and cut into squares to serve.

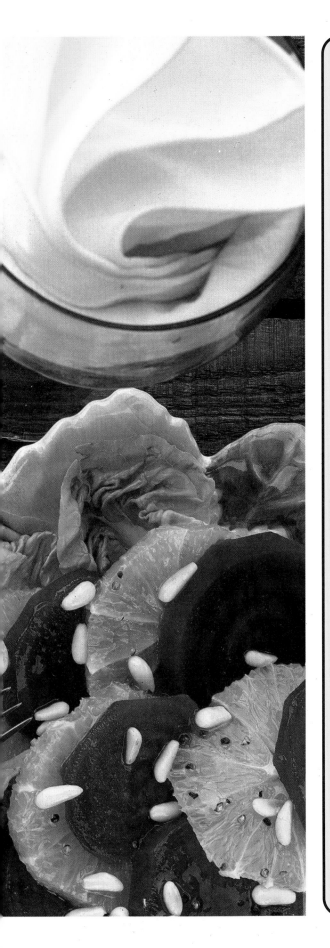

Marilyn Hansen

Menu 1
(*left*)
Beef Stroganoff with Kasha
Beetroot and Oranges Vinaigrette

Marilyn Hansen cites her extensive world travels as the major influence on her cooking. Wherever she visits, she makes a point of going to local restaurants and wineries and of collecting recipes from native cooks. When cooking at home, she often streamlines and lightens traditional recipes to save time and to suit diet-conscious friends. In the three menus she presents here, she gives new twists to classic international recipes.

The highlight of Menu 1 is the Russian favourite beef Stroganoff, sautéed strips or cubes of beef in a rich sour-cream-based sauce. Here Marilyn Hansen reduces calories by substituting low-fat yogurt for some of the sour cream. *Kasha*, or buckwheat groats, and dark pumpernickel bread are served with the Stroganoff.

Bouillabaisse is the main course of Menu 2, an ideal buffet meal. In this prepare-ahead version of the classic French seafood stew, the cook uses several kinds of fish as well as shrimp and mussels. For an original touch, she adds curry powder instead of the usual saffron threads. Tomato aspic, flavoured with lemon juice and chutney and presented on a bed of watercress, is the salad.

In the Scandinavian-inspired Menu 3, Marilyn Hansen gives traditional Swedish meatballs new zest with allspice and caraway seeds. She cooks the meatballs in advance, then reheats them in a creamy but not overly heavy gravy before serving. Marinated cucumbers with sliced radishes and radish sprouts are the colourful complement.

Everyone will welcome this substantial cold-weather dinner of beef Stroganoff served with kasha *and buttered black bread. The light salad of beetroot and oranges is sprinkled with pine nuts.*

Beef Stroganoff with Kasha
Beetroot and Oranges Vinaigrette

For a more dramatic presentation, serve the beef Stroganoff in a bread 'tureen.' Select a dense 500 g (1 lb) round loaf of dark pumpernickel bread and, using a serrated knife, cut off a lid about 5 cm (2 inches) from the top of the loaf. With a spoon, scoop out the interior of the loaf to form a bowl, leaving the walls about 1¹/₂–2¹/₂ cm (³/₄–1 inch) thick. Wrap the bowl and its lid in a plastic bag until serving time. Just before serving, place the bowl and lid on a cookie sheet in a preheated 180°C (350°F or Mark 4) oven to warm for 10 minutes. Spoon the *kasha* onto a large platter. Place the bread tureen on the bed of *kasha* and fill it with Stroganoff. To serve, spoon the Stroganoff onto individual dinner plates and cut the bread into wedges.

What to drink

The cook suggests a robust wine to match the earthy flavours of this menu. A California Zinfandel, Cabernet Sauvignon, or Merlot would be equally good.

Start-to-Finish Steps

The day before or the morning of serving

1 Follow Stroganoff recipe steps 1 and 2 and salad recipe steps 1 through 5.
2 Follow Stroganoff recipe steps 3 through 6.

Fifteen minutes before serving

1 Follow kasha recipe steps 1 through 3 and Stroganoff recipe steps 7 and 8.
2 While kasha and Stroganoff are cooking, follow salad recipe step 6.
3 Follow kasha recipe steps 4 and 5.
4 Follow Stroganoff recipe steps 9 and 10 and serve with salad.

Beef Stroganoff with Kasha

750 g (1¹/₂ lb) boneless top sirloin steak cut 2¹/₂ cm (1 inch) thick, or flank steak
Medium-size onion
Small bunch scallions
Medium-size clove garlic
250 g (8 oz) white mushrooms
Small bunch dill
30 g (1 oz) capers
125 g (4 oz) canned pitted black olives
6 tablespoons unsalted butter, approximately
2 tablespoons vegetable oil
500 ml (1 pt) sour cream
250 ml (8 fl oz) low-fat yogurt
1¹/₂ teaspoons salt
¹/₂ teaspoon freshly ground black pepper
1 tablespoon Worcestershire sauce
125 g (4 oz) chèvre
Large loaf dark pumpernickel bread
Kasha (see following recipe)

1 Wrap beef in plastic or foil and place in freezer at least 30 minutes, or until partially frozen.
2 Meanwhile, peel onion and halve lengthwise. Cut into thin wedges; set aside. Wash, dry, and trim scallions. Cut enough scallions, including green tops, diagonally into 1 cm (¹/₂ inch) slices to measure about 100 g (3 oz). Peel and crush garlic. Wipe mushrooms clean with damp paper towels and slice thinly. Wash dill and pat dry. Wrap and refrigerate 4 sprigs for garnish and finely chop enough remaining dill to measure 30 g (1 oz). Drain capers. Drain olives and thinly slice.
3 When beef is firm, cut across grain into thin slices. Cut slices into 1 x 5 cm (¹/₂ x 2 inch) long strips.
4 In large deep heavy-gauge skillet, melt 1 tablespoon butter in 1 tablespoon oil over medium-high heat. Add one third of beef strips and sauté, stirring, about 2 minutes, or until browned. Using slotted spatula, transfer cooked beef to medium-size bowl. Sauté remaining beef in two batches and add to bowl.
5 Add onion to skillet and sauté, stirring, 2 minutes, or until slightly wilted; add to bowl with beef. Add remaining 1 tablespoon oil and 1 tablespoon butter to skillet along with scallions, garlic, and mushrooms, and sauté, stirring, 1 minute; add to beef.

6 Add sour cream, yogurt, chopped dill, salt, and pepper to skillet and cook, stirring, 2 minutes, or until almost boiling. (Do not allow mixture to boil.) Add Worcestershire sauce, capers, olives, and beef-onion mixture, and stir to blend. Return mixture to bowl, cover, and refrigerate until about 15 minutes before serving.

7 About 15 minutes before serving, turn Stroganoff into large heavy-gauge skillet and cook, stirring occasionally, 7 to 10 minutes, or until heated through. Do not allow Stroganoff to boil.

8 Meanwhile, cut chèvre into small cubes; set aside. Slice bread, and butter generously.

9 When Stroganoff is hot, stir in chèvre and mix gently; chèvre does not have to melt completely.

10 To serve, divide kasha among 4 dinner plates. Spoon Stroganoff over kasha and garnish with dill sprigs. Serve with buttered bread.

Kasha

750 ml (1 1/2 pts) beef stock
125 g (4 oz) medium or coarse kasha
1 egg
3/4 teaspoon salt
1/4 teaspoon freshly ground black pepper
Small bunch parsley
2 tablespoon unsalted butter

1 In medium-size saucepan, bring beef stock to a boil over high heat.

2 Meanwhile, combine kasha, egg, salt, and pepper in large heavy-gauge saucepan over low heat. Mix well and stir until kasha is dry.

3 When stock boils, add it to kasha mixture and cover pan. Reduce heat to medium-low and cook, stirring with fork once or twice, 7 to 10 minutes, or until kasha grains are tender.

4 Wash and dry parsley. Finely chop enough parsley to measure 15 g (1/2 oz).

5 Add parsley and butter to kasha, tossing with fork to combine. Cover and keep warm on stove top until ready to serve.

Beetroot and Oranges Vinaigrette

6 medium-size fresh beetroot (about 500 g (1 lb) total weight)
2 medium-size navel oranges or blood oranges
60 g (2 oz) pine nuts
100 ml (3 fl oz) vegetable oil
3 tablespoons white wine vinegar
2 teaspoons honey
1 teaspoon Dijon mustard
1/4 teaspoon salt
1/4 teaspoon freshly ground pepper
Large head lettuce or large bunch watercress

1 Bring 2 1/2 cm (1 inch) of water to a boil in large heavy-gauge saucepan. Meanwhile, wash beetroot, being careful not to damage skin. Trim beetroot tops, leaving 2 1/2 cm (1 inch) of tops attached. Place beetroot in vegetable steamer over boiling water, cover pan, and steam 15 to 20 minutes, or until tender.

2 Meanwhile, peel oranges, removing all white pith. Slice oranges crosswise into 5 mm (1/4 inch) slices, place in plastic bag, and refrigerate until ready to serve.

3 In small dry skillet, toast pine nuts over medium heat, stirring, about 2 minutes, or until lightly browned. Remove pan from heat; add oil, vinegar, honey, mustard, salt, and pepper, and stir to blend. Pour dressing into jar with tight-fitting lid and refrigerate until needed.

4 When beetroot is cooked, turn into colander and cool under cold running water; drain well. Slip off skins and cut into 5 mm (1/4 inch) slices. Place beetroot in plastic bag and refrigerate until needed.

5 Wash lettuce or watercress and dry in salad spinner or with paper towels. Wrap in dry paper towels, place in plastic bag, and refrigerate until needed.

6 Just before serving, make a bed of lettuce or watercress on each of 4 salad plates. Arrange beetroot and orange slices on greens. Shake salad dressing well to recombine, and drizzle some dressing over each salad.

Bouillabaisse with Croutons and Rouille
Tomato-Chutney Aspic

French cooks typically use saffron to colour and flavour their *bouillabaisse*. Here the cook substitutes curry powder, which is less costly and adds a subtle flavour all its own. If you prefer the more traditional seasoning, use $^1/_2$ teaspoon saffron threads in place of the curry powder. Let your guests spoon the *rouille* (garlic mayonnaise) over the *bouillabaisse* to suit their individual tastes.

Although it may sound tricky, making an aspic with unflavoured gelatin is quite simple. To get the best results, use only one envelope of gelatin; never try for a thicker aspic by adding more gelatin or the aspic will be rubbery. The aspic should be refrigerated until just before serving, and, if served as part of a buffet, should be presented on a chilled platter.

What to drink
This meal demands a crisp, well-chilled white wine. Try an Italian Pinot Grigio or Verdicchio.

Start-to-Finish Steps

The day before or the morning of serving
1 Peel garlic and mince enough to measure 1 tablespoon for bouillabaisse recipe and 1 tablespoon for rouille recipe. Halve 1 lemon and squeeze enough juice to measure 1 tablespoon each for rouille and aspic recipes.
2 Follow aspic recipe steps 1 through 4.
3 Follow bouillabaisse recipe steps 1 through 8.
4 Follow rouille recipe steps 1 and 2.

Fifteen minutes before serving
1 Follow rouille recipe step 3, bouillabaisse recipe steps 9 through 11, and aspic recipe step 5.
2 Follow bouillabaisse recipe steps 12 through 14 and aspic recipe step 6.
3 Follow bouillabaisse recipe steps 15 and 16 and serve with aspic.

Tempting bouillabaisse *with a peppery* rouille *makes an elegant meal at any time of year. Present the rectangles of shimmering tomato aspic with their yogurt-and-sour-cream topping on a bed of crisp watercress.*

Bouillabaisse with Croutons and Rouille

1 medium-size plus 1 small onion
Medium-size leek
2 medium-size stalks celery with leaves
Small fennel bulb
5 tablespoons good-quality olive oil
1 tablespoon minced garlic
1 Kg (2 lb) canned Italian plum tomatoes with juice
Small bunch fresh thyme, or $1/2$ teaspoon dried
1 teaspoon curry powder, or $1/2$ teaspoon saffron
    threads
$1/4$ teaspoon red pepper flakes
1 bay leaf
125 ml (4 fl oz) dry white wine or dry vermouth
2 teaspoons salt
Freshly ground black pepper
500 g (1 lb) medium-size shrimp
Three 250 ml (8 fl oz) bottles clam juice or 750 ml
    ($1^{1}/2$ pts) fish stock
250 g (8 oz) flounder or sole fillets
250 g (8 oz) catfish, yellow perch, or freshwater trout
    fillets, or salmon or cod steaks
250 g (8 oz) mussels (about 12)
Large loaf Italian or French bread
Small bunch parsley
1 tablespoon Sambuca or other anise-flavoured
    liqueur
Rouille (see following recipe)

1 Peel medium-size onion and finely chop enough to measure 125 g (4 oz). Reserve small onion. Trim root end from leek and split leek lengthwise. Wash leek thoroughly under cold running water to remove all grit and dry with paper towel. Discard dark green tops of leek and finely chop enough white and light green parts to measure 125 g (4 oz). Wash, dry, and trim celery. Finely chop enough celery stalks and leaves to measure 125 g (4 oz). Wash, dry, and trim fennel bulb. Finely chop enough fennel to measure 100 g (3 oz).

2 Heat 3 tablespoons olive oil over medium heat in large heavy-gauge non-aluminium stockpot or Dutch oven. Add chopped onion, leek, celery, fennel, and garlic, and sauté, stirring often, 5 minutes, or until softened.

3 Meanwhile, drain tomatoes in strainer over medium-size bowl; reserve juice. Coarsely chop tomatoes. Wash fresh thyme, if using, and dry with paper towels. Strip enough leaves from stems to measure 1 teaspoon.

4 Add tomatoes and their juice, thyme, curry powder, red pepper flakes, bay leaf, wine, salt, and pepper to taste to stockpot. Bring mixture to a boil, reduce heat to medium-low, cover, and simmer 15 minutes.

5 Meanwhile, peel and devein shrimp, *reserving* shells. Wrap and refrigerate shrimp until needed.

6 Place clam juice, shrimp shells, and small unpeeled onion in medium-size non-aluminium saucepan, and bring to a boil over high heat. Reduce heat to low and simmer 10 minutes.

7 Meanwhile, cut all fish fillets or steaks into 5 x $2^{1}/2$ cm (2 x 1 inch) pieces. Scrub mussels with stiff-bristled brush, remove hairlike beards, and rinse mussels under cold running water. Wrap fish and mussels in separate plastic bags and refrigerate until needed.

8 Strain broth, discard shrimp shells and onion, and add broth to tomato mixture. Stir to combine, cover, and refrigerate soup base until needed.

9 Fifteen minutes before serving, preheat oven to 200°C (400°F or Mark 6).

10 Bring soup to a boil over medium-high heat.

11 Cut bread into 1 cm ($1/2$ inch) slices and arrange in a single layer on large baking sheet.

12 Toast bread in oven about 7 minutes, or until lightly browned.

13 Meanwhile, add fish pieces, shrimp, and mussels to boiling soup base, reduce heat to medium-low, and simmer 3 to 4 minutes, or just until fish is opaque, shrimp turn pink, and mussels open.

14 Wash and dry parsley. Finely chop enough to measure 2 tablespoons.

15 Discard any mussels that have not opened. Add parsley, Sambuca, and remaining 2 tablespoons olive oil to soup. Taste, and adjust seasonings if necessary.

16 Ladle bouillabaisse into large tureen and serve with hot croutons and rouille. Let guests spoon rouille into stew or spread on croutons.

Rouille

250 g (8 oz) mayonnaise
2 tablespoons good-quality olive oil
1 tablespoon lemon juice
1 tablespoon minced garlic
1 teaspoon paprika
$1/2$ teaspoon salt
$1/4$ teaspoon hot pepper sauce

1 Combine all ingredients in food processor or blender. Process 5 seconds, or just until blended.

2 Turn rouille into small bowl, cover, and refrigerate until 15 minutes before serving.

3 Fifteen minutes before serving, set out rouille to come to room temperature.

Tomato-Chutney Aspic

1 sachet unflavoured gelatin
350 ml (12 fl oz) tomato juice
60 g (2 oz) mango chutney
1 tablespoon lemon juice
$^1/_2$ teaspoon Worcestershire sauce
$^1/_4$ teaspoon hot pepper sauce
175 g (6 fl oz) low-fat yogurt
4 tablespoons sour cream
$^1/_4$ teaspoon salt
Freshly ground pepper
Large bunch watercress
Medum-size lemon
100 g (3 oz) chopped walnuts

1 In small bowl, sprinkle gelatin over 2 tablespoons tomato juice and set aside to soften, about 5 minutes.

2 Meanwhile, place remaining tomato juice in medium-size non-aluminium saucepan. Add chutney, lemon juice, Worcestershire sauce, and hot pepper sauce. Bring to a boil over high heat. Add softened gelatin, reduce heat to low, and stir about 1 minute, or until gelatin dissolves. Pour mixture into small loaf pan, cover, and refrigerate until set, at least 2 hours.

3 In small bowl, combine yogurt, sour cream, salt, and pepper to taste and stir gently to blend. Cover and refrigerate until needed.

4 Wash watercress and dry in salad spinner or with paper towels. Place in plastic bag and refrigerate until needed.

5 Just before serving, arrange watercress on platter, reserving 4 sprigs for garnish. Wash and dry lemon and cut into thin wedges.

6 Cut aspic into 4 equal portions and use spatula to remove from pan. Place aspic on top of watercress. Spoon a dollop of yogurt mixture on top of each portion of aspic and sprinkle with walnuts. Garnish each with a sprig of watercress, and garnish platter with lemon wedges.

Swedish Meatballs
Cucumber and Radish Salad

For the best results in preparing the meatballs, follow these tips: Chill the ingredients thoroughly before shaping the balls. Moisten your hands with cold water before rolling the seasoned meat between your palms. Handle the meatballs gently so they will have a light texture. Turn the meatballs once during baking to keep them nicely rounded.

What to drink

A full-bodied imported beer suits this simple Scandinavian dinner. Alternatively, select a full-bodied and flavourful white wine, such as a California Chardonnay or a French Saint-Véran.

Flavourful Swedish meatballs and a refreshing salad of thinly sliced cucumbers and radishes is an easy meal for family or company.

Start-to-Finish Steps

The day before or the morning of serving

1 Follow salad recipe steps 1 and 2.
2 Follow meatballs recipe steps 1 through 8.
3 Follow salad recipe steps 3 and 4.

Fifteen minutes before serving

1 Follow meatballs recipe step 9.
2 While meatballs are reheating, follow salad recipe steps 5 through 7.
3 Follow meatballs recipe steps 10 and 11 and serve with salad.

Swedish Meatballs

Meatballs:
Medium-size onion
1 tablespoon unsalted butter
3 to 4 slices firm home-style white bread
125 ml (4 fl oz) cold milk
1½ teaspoons salt
½ teaspoon freshly ground black pepper
1 teaspoon caraway seeds
½ teaspoon ground allspice
1 egg
500 g (1 lb) lean minced beef, well chilled
250 g (8 oz) lean minced pork, well chilled

Gravy:
2 tablespoons unsalted butter
2 tablespoons plain flour
1 cup half-and-half milk and cream
175 ml (6 fl oz) beef stock
1 teaspoon Worcestershire sauce
1 teaspoon meat extract paste (optional)
Salt and freshly ground black pepper
Small bunch parsley for garnish

1 Preheat oven to 200°C (400°F or Mark 6). Line roasting pan with foil.
2 For meatballs, peel onion and finely chop enough to measure 60 g (2 oz). In small skillet, melt butter over medium heat. Add onion and sauté 5 minutes, or until tender.
3 Meanwhile, trim crusts from bread. Using coarse side of grater, grate enough bread to measure 100 g (3 oz) crumbs. In large bowl, combine onion, bread crumbs, milk, salt, pepper, caraway seeds, allspice, and egg; mix well.
4 Add beef and pork to onion mixture; combine well.
5 Using about a teaspoonful of mixture for each

meatball, shape meat with hands into about 40 small meatballs and place in foil-lined roasting pan.
6 Bake meatballs, turning once, 12 to 15 minutes, or until meatballs are cooked through and firm when pressed.
7 Turn meatballs into medium-size bowl, cover, and refrigerate until 15 minutes before serving.
8 For gravy, in large skillet, melt butter over medium heat. Add flour and stir until smooth. Add half-and-half and stock and bring to a boil, whisking constantly. Cook mixture, continuing to whisk, 5 minutes, or until gravy thickens. Whisk in Worcestershire sauce, meat extract paste if using, and salt and pepper to taste. Pour gravy into small bowl, cover, and refrigerate until 15 minutes before serving.
9 Fifteen minutes before serving, pour gravy into large deep skillet or flameproof casserole. Add meatballs and bring gravy to a boil over medium-high heat. Reduce heat to medium-low, cover, and simmer 10 minutes, or until meatballs are heated through. (If necessary, you may hold meatballs and gravy in covered skillet or casserole in preheated moderate oven until ready to serve.)
10 Just before serving, wash and dry parsley. Chop enough parsley to measure 1 teaspoon.
11 Divide meatballs and gravy among 4 dinner plates and sprinkle with chopped parsley.

Cucumber and Radish Salad

2 medium-size cucumbers (about 500 g (1 lb) total weight), plus 1 large cucumber for garnish (optional)
3 teaspoons salt
Large bunch red radishes
175 ml (6 fl oz) white wine vinegar or rice vinegar
3 tablespoons sugar
½ teaspoon freshly ground black pepper
Small package radish sprouts or small bunch watercress
Small bunch dill

1 Peel medium-size cucumbers and cut crosswise into very thin slices.
2 Place half of cucumber slices in glass pie plate and sprinkle with 1 teaspoon salt. Top with remaining cucumber slices and 1 teaspoon salt. Cover with heavy plate to press out excess water. Set cucumbers aside for 20 to 30 minutes.
3 Trim radishes and cut crosswise into very thin

slices. Place in plastic bag and refrigerate until needed.

4 For dressing, in medium-size non-aluminium bowl, combine vinegar, sugar, remaining teaspoon salt, and pepper. Drain cucumbers and add to dressing; cover and refrigerate until needed.

5 Just before serving, wash and dry radish sprouts and dill; chop enough to measure 2 tablespoons each. If using cucumber for garnish, cut into fans.

6 Pour off and discard most of dressing. Add radishes, radish sprouts, and dill to cucumbers and mix gently.

7 Divide salad among 4 dinner plates. Garnish each plate with a cucumber fan, if desired.

Added touch

This pie is a fitting conclusion to a cold-weather meal. Adjust the amount of maple syrup and the baking time to the sweetness and ripeness of the pears.

Deep-Dish Pear Pie

Pastry:
175 g (6 oz) unsifted plain flour
1/2 teaspoon salt
60 g (2 oz) lard, well chilled
2 tablespoons unsalted butter, well chilled
60 ml (2 fl oz) ice water

Filling:
1 1/4 Kg (2 1/2 lb) medium-ripe pears, such as Comice or Anjou
2 tablespoons plain flour
2 tablespoons unsalted butter

125–250 ml (4–8 fl oz) maple syrup
1/4 teaspoon salt
1/4 teaspoon freshly grated nutmeg
1/4 teaspoon ground cinnamon

Glaze:
1 tablespoon milk
1 tablespoon sugar

1 Preheat oven to 220°C (425°F or Mark 7).

2 Prepare pastry: In large bowl, combine flour and salt. Using pastry blender or 2 knives, cut in shortening and butter until mixture resembles coarse cornmeal.

3 Sprinkle ice water over mixture and stir with fork until dough forms a ball and pulls away from sides of bowl. Cover and refrigerate while making filling.

4 Prepare filling: Peel halve, and core pears. Cut crosswise into 1 cm (1/2 inch) slices and place in large bowl.

5 Blend flour with 1 tablespoon butter and add in bits to pears.

6 Add maple syrup to taste, salt, nutmeg, and cinnamon; stir to mix. Pour filling into deep 22 1/2 cm (9 inch) pie pan or 25 cm (10 inch) gratin dish. Dot with remaining 1 tablespoon butter.

7 On floured board, roll out pastry to size of pan plus 1 cm (1/2 inch). Cover pears and turn under overhanging pastry. Flute edge and cut several steam vents in pastry. Brush pastry with milk and sprinkle with sugar.

8 Bake pie on middle rack of oven 30 to 45 minutes, or until crust is golden brown and filling is bubbling. Serve warm.

Margaret Fraser

Menu 1
(*right*)
Taramosalata with Crudités and Pitta Bread
Lamb Kebabs
Stuffed Tomatoes

According to Margaret Fraser, Greek immigrants settling throughout Canada have contributed generously to the cuisine of their adopted homeland. Greek markets attract the uninitiated and curious with lavish displays of such delicacies as grape leaves in brine, barrels of oil-cured olives, bundles of dried herbs, and trays of sugar-dusted pastries. 'As a result of this exposure,' says Margaret Fraser, 'we Canadian cooks are adding more and more Greek dishes to our repertoires.' The three menus she presents here are all easily assembled Greek meals.

In Menu 1, a number of popular Greek seasonings flavour the dishes: lemon juice in the *taramosalata* (fish roe dip); garlic and rosemary in the marinade for the lamb kebabs; and oregano in the rice-stuffed tomatoes. You can serve the *taramosalata* as an appetizer, but if you do, the cook suggests that you leave it on the table during the meal to eat with the pitta.

The *spanakopita*, or spinach pie, of Menu 2 consists of layers of flaky filo pastry enfolding a spinach and feta cheese filling. Although it may appear difficult to make, the pie can be prepared quickly once you master handling the filo dough. As accompaniments, Margaret Fraser serves a chilled version of the lemon soup known in Greece as *avgolemono*, and a salad of marinated artichokes and olives.

Originally a Middle Eastern dish, the *moussaka* of Menu 3 was long ago adopted by the Greeks. This hearty eggplant and ground lamb casserole goes well with a simple lettuce salad. Melon balls with *ouzo* cream are the light dessert.

Casual ceramics suit this bright Greek meal of taramosalata with crudités and toasted pitta triangles, broiled lamb kebabs, and tomatoes filled with herbed rice.

Taramosalata with Crudités and Pitta Bread
Lamb Kebabs
Stuffed Tomatoes

The popular Greek appetizer taramosalata, known as 'poor man's caviar,' is a creamy purée most often served as a dip or spread. It is usually made from the tiny orange eggs, or roe (tarama), of carp, although occasionaly tuna or gray mullet roe is used. Look for tarama in bottles in Greek and Middle Eastern markets or in speciality food shops. If you are on a salt-restricted diet, soak the tarama in water for 5 to 10 minutes, then drain it well. Tarama keps in the refrigerator for up to three months; taramosalata can be made up to five days in advance of serving and stored in the refrigerator.

What to drink
A Cabernet Sauvignon is always a good choice with lamb. Try a young California Cabernet or one from the Médoc region.

Start-to-Finish Steps

The day before or the morning of serving
1   Wash 2 lemons and dry with paper towels. Halve lemons. Cut 3 thick slices from one half for kebabs recipe. Squeeze enough juice from remaining

halves to measure ¼ cup for taramosalata recipe. Crush and peel 4 cloves garlic for kebabs recipe. Peel and mince remaining clove for stuffed tomatoes recipe.
2   Follow stuffed tomatoes recipe step 1.
3   Follow kebabs recipe steps 1 and 2.
4   Follow stuffed tomatoes recipe steps 2 through 8.
5   While tomatoes are baking, follow taramosalata recipe steps 1 through 4.

Thirty minutes before serving
1   Follow kebabs recipe step 3, stuffed tomatoes recipe step 9, and taramosalata recipe step 5.
2   Follow kebabs recipe steps 4 through 6.
3   While kebabs are broiling, follow taramosalata recipe steps 6 through 9.
4   Follow stuffed tomatoes recipe step 10, kebabs recipe step 7, and serve with taramosalata.

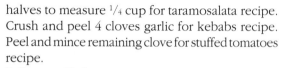

Taramosalata with Crudités and Pitta Bread

3 thick slices home-style white bread
Small onion
100 g (3 oz) tarama
4 tablespoons lemon juice
½ teaspoon salt
Freshly ground pepper
125 ml (4 fl oz) good-quality olive oil
Large courgette
Large red bell pepper
Two 10 cm (6 inch) pitta breads

1   Place white bread on plate, pour 175 ml (6 fl oz) water over bread, and let soak 10 minutes.
2   Meanwhile, peel and coarsely chop onion. In food processor or blender, combine onion, tarama, lemon juice, salt, and pepper to taste. Process until combined.
3   Gently squeeze out excess water from bread and tear bread into chunks. Add to food processor or blender and process until smooth.
4   With machine running, add olive oil in a slow, steady stream. Process until mixture is smooth and light pink in colour. Transfer to small serving

bowl, cover, and refrigerate until 30 minutes before serving.

5 Thirty minutes before serving, set out taramosalata to come to room temperature.

6 Wash courgette and bell pepper and dry with paper towels. Trim courgette and cut crosswise into 5 mm ($^1/_4$ inch) slices. Core and seed bell pepper; cut into 2$^1/_2$ cm (1 inch) squares.

7 Cut each pitta bread into 6 wedges.

8 Five minutes before serving, wrap pitta wedges in foil and warm in broiler or very hot oven 2 to 3 minutes. Place in napkin-lined basket to keep warm.

9 Divide courgette slices and bell pepper squares among 4 salad plates and serve with taramosalata and pitta.

Lamb Kebabs

Small bunch fresh rosemary, or 2 teaspoons dried
3 thick slices lemon, plus 1 lemon for garnish
4 medium-size cloves garlic, crushed and peeled
125 ml (4 fl oz) good-quality olive oil
Salt and freshly ground pepper
850 g (1$^3/_4$ lb) lean boneless lamb, cut into 2$^1/_2$ cm (1 inch) cubes

1 Wash fresh rosemary, if using, and pat dry with paper towels. Reserve 4 sprigs for garnish. Mince enough remaining rosemary to measure 2 tablespoons.

2 Combine lemon slices, fresh or dried rosemary, garlic, olive oil, and salt and pepper to taste in shallow glass or ceramic dish. Add lamb, cover with plastic wrap, and refrigerate, turning lamb occasionally, at least 2 hours or overnight.

3 Thirty minutes before serving, preheat broiler. Remove lamb from refrigerator.

4 Wash and dry lemon for garnish. Cut into 12 wedges; set aside.

5 Remove lamb from marinade and thread onto four 25–30 cm (10–12 inch) skewers. Arrange skewers in broiler pan.

6 Broil kebabs about 10 cm (6 inches) from heat, turning occasionally and brushing generously with marinade, 12 minutes, or until browned.

7 Transfer kebabs to dinner plates and garnish with lemon wedges, and rosemary sprigs if desired.

Stuffed Tomatoes

4 medium-size tomatoes (about 750 g (1½ lb) total weight)
Salt
60 g (2 oz) long-grain white rice
2 tablespoons pine nuts
2 tablespoons good-quality olive oil
Medium-size clove garlic, minced
¼ teaspoon dried thyme
¼ teaspoon dried oregano
Small bunch chives for garnish (optional)

1 Preheat oven to 190°C (375°F or Mark 5). Lightly grease shallow 1-quart baking dish.
2 Bring 175 ml (6 fl oz) water to a boil over high heat in small saucepan.
3 Wash tomatoes and dry with paper towels. Cut tops off tomatoes. Scoop out and reserve pulp; remove and discard seeds. Lightly salt insides of tomato shells and invert on paper towels to drain.
4 Add rice to boiling water, cover, and cook over medium-low heat 20 minutes, or until tender.

5 Meanwhile, brown pine nuts in small dry skillet over medium heat 3 to 4 minutes, stirring constantly. Transfer pine nuts to small bowl and set aside.
6 Heat oil in skillet over medium heat until hot. Add garlic, thyme, oregano, and reserved tomato pulp and cook 3 to 4 minutes, or until excess liquid has evaporated. Remove skillet from heat and stir in rice and pine nuts.
7 Place tomato shells in prepared baking dish and spoon stuffing into shells.
8 Bake tomatoes 15 to 20 minutes, or until stuffing is lightly browned. Let tomatoes cool slightly, then cover and refrigerate until 30 minutes before serving.
9 Thirty minutes before serving, remove tomatoes from refrigerator to come to room temperature. Wash chives, if using, and dry with paper towels. Mince enough chives to measure 1 tablespoon; reserve remainder for another use.
10 Sprinkle tomatoes with chives, if desired, and transfer to dinner plates.

Chilled Avgolemono
Spanakopita
Marinated Artichokes with Greek Olives

Offer the delicate lemon and egg soup before or with the spanakopita *and the salad of marinated artichokes and olives.*

The spinach and feta cheese filling for the spanakopita is wrapped in filo, tissue-thin pastry sheets that are sold frozen. To prevent the sheet from cracking when you separate them, thaw the entire block of frozen filo in the refrigerator overnight. Never refreeze the extra dough or the sheets may stick together; refrigerate it and use it within a week.

Because filo becomes crumbly when exposed to air, work quickly and have your other ingredients ready before unrolling the dough. Unroll the dough and place eight sheets, unseparated, on a damp kitchen towel covered with plastic wrap; cover the top sheet with another piece of plastic wrap and a second damp towel. Work with one sheet of dough at a time, leaving the rest covered. The butter you brush on the sheets helps to separate the layers and turn the pastry a golden brown as it bakes. But take care – too much butter will make the pastry soggy. If feta cheese is unavailable, substitute a creamy chèvre or plain cream cheese. The flavour of the finished dish will not be as tangy, but it will still be good.

What to drink
A crisp, dry, flavourful white wine, such as a French Sancerre or a Sauvignon Blanc from California or Italy, goes best with these dishes.

Start-to-Finish Steps

The morning of serving
1 Wash 2 lemons and dry with paper towels. Halve 1 lemon for artichokes recipe. Squeeze enough juice from remaining lemon to measure $1/3$ cup and set aside for avgolemono recipe.
2 Follow spanakopita recipe steps 1 and 2.
3 Follow avgolemono recipe steps 1 and 2 and artichokes recipe steps 1 through 3.
4 Follow avgolemono recipe step 3.
5 While rice is cooking, follow artichokes recipe step 4 and spanakopita recipe step 3.
6 Follow avgolemono recipe step 4 and spanakopita recipe step 4.
7 Follow artichokes recipe steps 5 and 6.
8 Follow spanakopita recipe steps 5 through 10.

About thirty minutes before serving
1 Follow spanakopita recipe steps 11 and 12.
2 Toward end of spanakopita baking time, follow artichokes recipe steps 7 and 8 and avgolemono recipe steps 5 and 6.
3 Follow spanakopita recipe step 13 and serve with avgolemono and artichokes.

Chilled Avgolemono

1 ltr (1$3/4$ pts) chicken stock
Small bunch mint
60 g (2 oz) long-grain white rice
2 eggs
100 ml (3 fl oz) lemon juice
Salt and freshly ground white pepper
Large lemon for garnish

1 Bring stock to a boil in medium-size saucepan over high heat.
2 Meanwhile, wash mint and pat dry with paper towels. Enclose 4 sprigs mint in small square of cheesecloth and tie securely with kitchen string. Wrap remaining mint in plastic and reserve.
3 Add cheesecloth packet and rice to stock. Reduce heat to medium-low, cover, and cook 15 to 20 minutes, or until rice is tender. Discard cheesecloth packet.
4 In large non-aluminium bowl, beat eggs with whisk until light and frothy. Add hot stock and rice very slowly, whisking constantly. (If stock is added too quickly, eggs will curdle.) Stir in lemon juice, and salt and pepper to taste. Cover bowl with plastic wrap and refrigerate until just before serving.
5 Just before serving, wash lemon and dry with paper towel. Cut 4 thin slices for garnish. Finely chop enough reserved mint to measure 1 teaspoon.
6 Divide soup among 4 bowls and garnish each with a lemon slice and some chopped mint.

Spanakopita

Small bunch dill
125 g (4 oz) fresh mushrooms
Medium-size onion
500 g (1 lb) spinach
7 tablespoons unsalted butter
3 eggs
250 g (8 oz) feta cheese
$^1/_2$ teaspoon each dried oregano and thyme
$^1/_2$ teaspoon salt
8 sheets frozen filo dough, thawed

1 Wash dill and pat dry with paper towels. Finely chop enough dill to measure 2 tablespoons. Wipe mushrooms clean with damp paper towels and chop finely. Peel and finely chop onion.

2 Wash spinach in several changes of cold water. Do not dry. Remove tough stems and discard.

3 Place spinach in large saucepan and cook, covered, over medium-high heat 3 to 5 minutes, or until just wilted. Turn spinach into colander and refresh under cold running water. Drain well, pressing out excess moisture with back of spoon. Finely chop spinach; set aside.

4 Melt 2 tablespoons butter in large skillet over medium heat. Add onion and mushrooms and cook 3 minutes, or until soft. Remove from heat and add spinach; stir to combine and allow to cool 10 minutes.

5 Beat eggs lightly in small bowl and add to spinach mixture. Crumble in feta and add chopped dill, oregano, thyme, and salt. Set aside.

6 Melt remaining 5 tablespoons butter in small saucepan.

7 Butter bottom and sides of 20 cm (8 inch) square baking pan. Brush 1 sheet of filo lightly on one side with melted butter. Fold sheet to 20 cm (8 inch) width so that when placed in pan it completely covers bottom and overhangs evenly on two opposite sides.

8 Rotate pan a quarter turn and repeat procedure with another sheet of buttered filo. Repeat with 4 more sheets of filo, rotating pan a quarter turn each time. (Filo should hang over edges of pan on all four sides.)

9 Spread spinach-cheese filling over filo, smoothing top. One side at a time, fold overhanging filo over filling.

10 Cut remaining 2 sheets of filo into four 20 cm (8 inch) squares. Layer squares on top of filled pastry, brushing each square with melted butter before placing the next on top. Score top of spanakopita with sharp paring knife just through pastry layers (dividing it into 4 quarters) to ensure neat portions after baking. Cover with plastic wrap and refrigerate until 30 minutes before serving.

11 About 30 minutes before serving, preheat oven to 190°C (375°F or Mark 5).

12 Bake spanakopita 30 minutes, or until golden brown.

13 Cut spanakopita into four pieces and transfer to dinner plates.

Marinated Artichokes with Greek Olives

8 to 10 fresh baby artichokes (about 350 g (12 oz) total weight), or two large cans water-packed artichoke hearts
Small bunch fresh rosemary, or 1 teaspoon dried
Large lemon, halved
125 ml (4 fl oz) good-quality olive oil
Freshly ground black pepper
125 g (4 oz) small Greek olives

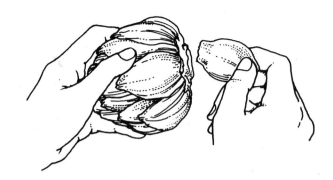

1 Bring 750 ml (1¹/₂ pts) water to a boil in medium-size saucepan.
2 Meanwhile, wash fresh artichokes and fresh rosemary, if using, and pat dry with paper towels. Roughly chop enough rosemary to measure 1 tablespoon and reserve remaining rosemary for another use. Pull off and discard any discoloured leaves from artichokes and trim stems. Using kitchen scissors, cut off tips of remaining leaves and rub cut surfaces with 1 lemon half.
3 If using canned artichokes, rinse and drain in colander, and sprinkle with juice from lemon half, if desired.
4 Add used lemon half and fresh artichokes to boiling water. Cover pan and simmer gently over medium-low heat 15 minutes, or until artichokes are tender when stems are pierced with a fork.
5 Combine olive oil, fresh or dried rosemary, and pepper to taste in large non-aluminium bowl. Cut remaining lemon half into 3 or 4 slices and add to bowl.
6 Drain fresh artichokes in colander and halve lengthwise. Add fresh or canned artichokes to marinade, cover bowl with plastic wrap, and refrigerate until 30 minutes before serving, stirring occasionally.
7 Just before serving, drain olives in strainer.
8 Using slotted spoon, transfer artichokes to salad plates. Divide olives among plates and serve.

<table>
<tr>
<td>
Menu

3
</td>
<td>

Moussaka
Lettuce with Cucumber-Yogurt Dressing
Sesame Pitta Crisps/Melon with Ouzo Cream

</td>
</tr>
</table>

The moussaka, with its custardy topping, is an excellent make-ahead dish that improves in flavour the longer it stands. Whether you bake it ahead and reheat it or refrigerate the unbaked dish to cook at mealtime, you will get fine results. The eggplants you choose should have smooth, glossy, unblemished skin. They should be firm and feel heavy for their size.

The Greek liqueur ouzo, used in the whipped cream for the fruit dessert, is a colourless, licorice-flavoured beverage brewed from grape extracts and aromatic plants.

What to drink
A zesty, reasonably full-bodied red wine will stand up best to the lively flavours of this meal. A young California Zinfandel is an excellent choice.

Start-to-Finish Steps

The day before or the morning of serving
1   Peel garlic and mince 2 cloves for moussaka recipe, 1 clove for lettuce recipe, and 1 clove for pitta recipe. Set out butter to come to room temperature for pitta recipe.
2   Follow melon recipe step 1, pitta recipe step 1, and moussaka recipe step 1.
3   Follow lettuce recipe step 1 and melon recipe step 2.
4   Follow pitta recipe steps 2 through 5.
5   Follow moussaka recipe steps 2 through 8.
6   Follow lettuce recipe steps 2 and 3 and melon recipe step 3.
7   Follow moussaka recipe steps 9 through 11.

Thirty minutes before serving
1   Follow pitta recipe step 6 and moussaka recipe steps 12 and 13.
2   Follow pitta recipe step 7.
3   Follow lettuce recipe step 4, pitta recipe step 8, and serve with moussaka.
4   Follow melon recipe steps 4 and 5 and serve for dessert.

For an informal buffet serve moussaka *hot from the oven, toasted pitta triangles, a green salad, and melon balls with* ouzo cream.

Moussaka

2 medium-size eggplants (about 850 g (1¾ lb) total weight)
4 teaspoons salt, approximately
Medium-size green bell pepper
Medium-size red bell pepper
Hot cherry pepper (optional)
2 medium-size onions
100 g (3 oz) Parmesan cheese
175 ml (6 fl oz) good-quality olive oil, approximately
2 medium-size cloves garlic, minced
250 g (8 oz) lean minced lamb
2 tablespoons tomato paste
1 teaspoon dried oregano
½ teaspoon dried basil
Freshly ground black pepper
60 g (2 oz) plain flour

Béchamel Sauce:
2 tablespoons unsalted butter
2 tablespoons plain flour
500 ml (1 pt) milk
2 eggs
½ teaspoon salt
Freshly ground white pepper

1 Wash eggplants and dry with paper towels. Trim but do not peel eggplants; cut crosswise into 1 cm (½ inch) slices. Sprinkle slices with 4 teaspoons salt and allow to drain in colander 20 minutes.
2 Wash peppers and dry with paper towels. Halve, core, and seed bell peppers and cut into thin strips. If using cherry pepper, seed and chop finely.

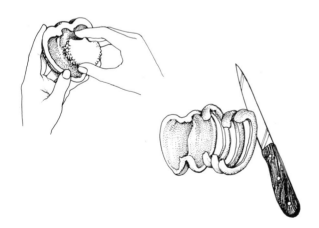

3 Peel and coarsely chop onions; you should have about 150 g (5 oz).
4 Using food processor or grater, grate enough Parmesan to measure 100 g (3 oz); set aside.
5 Heat 2 tablespoons olive oil in large skillet over medium heat until hot. Add peppers, onions, and garlic and cook 4 minutes, or until soft but not

brown. Using slotted spoon transfer vegetables to large bowl.
6 Add lamb to skillet and cook over medium-high heat, stirring often to break up any lumps, 5 minutes, or until meat is no longer pink.
7 Drain off excess fat. Return cooked vegetables to skillet with lamb and add tomato paste, oregano, basil, Parmesan, and black pepper to taste. Stir to combine well. Transfer mixture to large bowl and wipe skillet with paper towels.
8 Spread 60 g (2 oz) flour on sheet of waxed paper. Line large platter with paper towels. Heat 2 tablespoons olive oil in large skillet over medium-high heat until hot. Pat eggplant dry with paper towels and dredge slices lightly in flour. In batches, cook eggplant on both sides in skillet, adding more oil as necessary, 4 minutes, or until slightly browned. Transfer eggplant to paper-towel-lined platter.
9 For béchamel sauce, melt butter in small heavy-gauge non-aluminium saucepan over medium heat. Whisk in flour and cook, whisking continuously, 1 minute, or until bubbly. Gradually add milk and cook, stirring constantly, 3 to 5 minutes, or until mixture comes to a boil. Remove pan from heat.
10 Beat eggs in small bowl. Gradually add 125 ml (4 fl oz) hot milk mixture to eggs, stirring to combine well. Add egg mixture to saucepan and cook over low heat 1 minute. Add salt, and white pepper to taste.
11 Grease bottom and sides of large casserole or baking dish. Overlapping eggplant slices slightly, arrange half of eggplant in bottom of casserole. Cover with lamb mixture. Top with remaining eggplant. Pour béchamel sauce over eggplant and sprinkle with remaining Parmesan. Cover and refrigerate until 30 minutes before serving.
12 About 30 minutes before serving, preheat oven to 190°C (375°F or Mark 5).
13 Bake moussaka 30 minutes, or until sauce is bubbly and golden.

Lettuce with Cucumber-Yogurt Dressing

Small cucumber
1 teaspoon salt
125 ml (4 fl oz) plain yogurt
Medium-size clove garlic, minced
2 tablespoons good-quality olive oil
Freshly ground black pepper
Small head lettuce

1 Peel cucumber. Using grater, coarsely shred enough cucumber to measure 60 g (2 oz). Reserve remainder for another use. Place shredded cucumber in strainer, sprinkle with salt, and set aside to drain at leat 20 minutes.

2 After draining, combine cucumber, yogurt, garlic, olive oil, and pepper to taste in small bowl. Cover and refrigerate until just before serving.

3 Wash and dry lettuce. Discard any bruised or discoloured leaves and tear remaining lettuce into bite-size pieces. Wrap in paper towels, place in plastic bag, and refrigerate until just before serving.

4 To serve, place lettuce in salad bowl, add dressing, and toss.

Sesame Pitta Crisps

Three 10 cm (6 inch) pitta breads
Small lemon
4 tablespoons unsalted butter, at room temperature
2 teaspoons sesame seeds
Medium-size clove garlic, minced
1 teaspoon dried thyme

1 Preheat oven to 180°C (350°F or Mark 4).

2 Split each pitta bread to form 2 rounds and quarter each round. Place pitta on baking sheet and bake 7 to 8 minutes, or until dried. Remove from oven and let cool.

3 Meanwhile, halve lemon and squeeze enough juice to measure 1 tablespoon.

4 In small bowl, cream butter with sesame seeds, garlic, lemon juice, and thyme. Cover and refrigerate until 30 minutes before serving.

5 Place cooled pitta in plastic bag until needed.

6 Thirty minutes before serving, set out butter mixture to come to room temperature.

7 Spread pitta triangles with butter mixture and place on baking sheet.

8 Bake pitta triangles in 180°C (350°F or Mark 4) oven 4 to 5 minutes, or until crisp and golden.

Melon with Ouzo Cream

Small cantaloupe
Small honeydew melon
250 ml (8 fl oz) heavy cream
2 tablespoons brown sugar
2 tablespoons ouzo
Small bunch mint for garnish (optional)

1 Place large bowl and beaters in freezer to chill.

2 Halve and seed melons. Using small melon baller, scoop out enough balls from each melon to measure a total of 350 g (12 oz). Place a serving bowl, cover, and refrigerate until 30 minutes before serving.

3 Remove bowl and beaters from freezer. Beat cream in chilled bowl with electric mixer 2 minutes, or until soft peaks form. Add brown sugar and ouzo and beat until stiff peaks form. Cover and refrigerate until ready to serve.

4 Just before serving, wash and dry 2 large mint sprigs, if using; reserve remaining mint for another use.

5 If cream has separated, whisk briefly to recombine. Top melon balls with cream and garnish with mint sprigs.

Roberta Rall

Menu 1
(*left*)
Spinach and Potato Soup
Salmon and Pasta Sunburst Salad with
Herbed Mustard Sauce

Home economist Roberta Rall asks herself three questions when she develops recipes: Does the recipe make efficient use of time and ingredients? Can the recipe teach the cook a new skill? And can the recipe, if complicated, be simplified so that even an inexperienced cook can prepare it? In the salmon and pasta salad of Menu 1, for example, she cooks the pasta in the same cooking liquid used for poaching the salmon. The herbed mustard sauce that dresses the salad doubles as a dip for the accompanying artichoke leaves.

In Menu 2, Roberta Rall marinates the seafood Provençal all day in the same parchment paper in which it is baked. 'You can wrap the ingredients to be cooked in the parchment ahead of time,' she says, 'and the parchment will not get soggy.' With the seafood she offers potato pancakes, which she reheats in the oven at the last minute to give them a crisp, golden crust.

Menu 3 features *raclette*, a cheese-and-vegetable dish traditionally prepared by melting a half wheel of cheese near an open fire, then scraping the softened cheese over vegetables. Here the cook melts the cheese in a saucepan with butter, flour, and seasonings, pours it over individual casseroles of vegetables and ham, the bakes the casseroles. With the *raclette* she serves a salad of sugar snap peas, mushrooms, and radishes, and for dessert, fruit wrapped and baked in filo dough.

Spinach and potato soup garnished with scallion greens and lemon rind complements a lavish salad of pasta and salmon surrounded by artichoke leaves.

Spinach and Potato Soup
Salmon and Pasta Sunburst Salad with Herbed Mustard Sauce

The showy salad makes full use of the artichoke: The hearts are chopped and mixed with the pasta and salmon, and the leaves form an attractive, edible sunburst around the pasta. Select firm, compact artichokes with fleshly leaves that close tightly around the central choke. To store artichokes, wrap them unwashed in a damp towel, then in a plastic bag, and refrigerate them for up to two days.

What to drink

A bright and acidic white wine is called for here. Choose a Sauvignon Blanc from California or Italy, or a Pouilly-Fumé or Sancerre from France.

Start-to-Finish Steps

The morning of serving
1 Follow soup recipe steps 1 through 4.
2 While potato is cooking, follow salad recipe steps 1 through 5.
3 While salmon and artichoke are cooking, follow soup recipe steps 5 and 6.
4 Follow salad recipe steps 6 through 8.
5 While orzo is cooking, follow sauce recipe steps 1 and 2.
6 Follow salad recipe steps 9 and 10.

Fifteen minutes before serving
1 Follow salad recipe steps 11 through 14, soup recipe steps 7 and 8, and serve.

Spinach and Potato Soup

Medium-size new potato (about 175 g (6 oz))
4 medium-size scallions
Small lemon
500 g (1 lb) spinach
Small bunch mint
2 tablespoons unsalted butter
250 ml (8 fl oz) chicken stock
$^{1}/_{8}$ teaspoon nutmeg
$^{1}/_{4}$ teaspoon freshly ground white pepper
300 ml (10 fl oz) light cream

1 Scrub and rinse potato; do not peel. Wash scallions and lemon and dry with paper towels. Cut potato into 1 cm ($^{1}/_{2}$ inch) dice. Reserve one scallion for

garnish. Cut enough remaining scallions into 5 cm (2 inch) pieces to measure 100 g (3 oz). Using sharp paring knife, remove two 2$^{1}/_{2}$ cm (1 inch) wide strips of lemon rind; wrap and reserve for garnish. Halve lemon and squeeze enough juice to measure 2 teaspoons.

2 Remove and discard tough stems from spinach. Wash spinach in several changes of cold water and dry in salad spinner or with paper towels. Wash and dry mint; set aside 15 g ($^{1}/_{2}$ oz) loosely packed mint leaves.

Fresh mint

3 Melt butter in heavy-gauge stockpot over medium heat. Add scallion pieces and cook 2 minutes.
4 Add potato, stock, and 250 ml (8 fl oz) hot water and bring to a boil. Cover pot and cook over medium heat 12 minutes, or until potato is just tender.
5 Add spinach and cook, covered, 3 minutes, or just until wilted. Transfer mixture to food processor or blender and add 3 tablespoons mint leaves, lemon juice, nutmeg, and pepper. Process briefly until smooth.
6 Pour mixture into large non-aluminium bowl and stir in cream. Cut remaining mint into thin strips and stir into soup. Cover bowl and refrigerate until just before serving.
7 Just before serving, cut green part of reserved scallion and lemon rind into thin strips.
8 Stir soup and divide among 4 soup bowls. Garnish with strips of scallion green and lemon rind.

Salmon and Pasta Sunburst Salad

Small lemon
Medium-size artichoke (about 350 g (12 oz))
750 g (1½ lb) salmon fillets, 2½ cm (1 inch) thick
125 ml (4 fl oz) dry white wine
½ teaspoon whole black peppercorns
1 bay leaf
½ teaspoon salt
175 g (6 oz) orzo, or other small-shape pasta
Herbed Mustard Sauce (see following recipe)
Medium-size tomato

1   Bring 2 ltrs (3 pts) water to a boil in large saucepan over high heat.
2   Meanwhile, cut waxed-paper disk to fit large non-aluminium skillet. Wash lemon and artichoke and dry with paper towels. Halve lemon and cut 1 half into slices. Set aside other half. Trim stem and tough outer leaves from artichoke.
3   Wipe salmon with damp paper towels. Combine 500 ml (1 pt) water, wine, lemon slices, peppercorns, bay leaf, and salt in large non-aluminium skillet. Bring mixture to a boil over high heat.
4   Add salmon and cover with waxed paper. Return liquid to a boil, reduce heat to medium, and poach salmon 12 to 15 minutes, or just until fish flakes.
5   Meanwhile, halve artichoke and rub cut surfaces with reserved lemon half. Add artichoke halves and lemon half to boiling water in large saucepan. Cover pan and cook artichoke over medium heat 10 minutes, or until tender when pierced near stem end with fork.
6   Drain artichoke halves, wrap tightly in plastic, and refrigerate until 15 minutes before serving.
7   Using slotted spatula, transfer salmon to plate to cool. Using slotted spoon, remove and discard lemon slices, peppercorns, and bay leaf from cooking liquid.
8   Add pasta to cooking liquid and bring to a boil over medium-high heat. Cook pasta, stirring occasionally, 10 to 12 minutes, or until tender. Add additional hot water if necessary.
9   Rinse pasta in colander under cold running water; drain. Turn pasta into large bowl, cover with plastic wrap, and refrigerate until 15 minutes before serving.
10 Skin salmon and break into bite-size chunks, discarding any bones. Cover with plastic wrap and refrigerate until 15 minutes before serving.
11 To serve, remove pasta from refrigerator. Fold in salmon and ⅔ cup herbed mustard sauce.
12 Remove leaves from artichoke halves and arrange around outside edge of serving platter. Remove and discard fuzzy choke from each half. Chop artichoke heart and add to salmon and pasta mixture. Mix gently with fork.
13 Wash and dry tomato. If making tomato rose for garnish, use sharp paring knife to peel tomato skin in one continuous 5 mm–1 cm (¼–½ inch) wide strip. Roll strip into rose shape. If not making rose, do not peel tomato. Cut tomato into 2½ cm (1 inch) pieces and add to salad.
14 Spoon salad onto centre of platter and garnish with tomato rose, if desired. Serve remaining herbed mustard sauce separately as dipping sauce for artichoke leaves.

Herbed Mustard Sauce

Small bunch parsley
Small bunch basil, dill, or mint
125 g (4 oz) coarse-grain Dijon mustard
125 ml (4 fl oz) vegetable oil
4 tablespoons white wine vinegar or balsamic vinegar
2 to 3 tablespoons brown sugar

1   Wash and dry herbs. Mince enough parsley to measure 15 g (½ oz). Mince enough basil, dill, or mint to measure 15 g (½ oz). Reserve remaining herbs for another use.
2   Combine herbs, mustard, oil, vinegar, and sugar in small bowl and whisk until smooth. Cover and refrigerate until 15 minutes before serving.

<table>
<tr><td>

Menu

2

</td><td>

Seafood Provençal in Parchment
Lacy Potato Pancakes
Honeydew-Avocado Salad

</td></tr>
</table>

Let your guests open their own individual packets of seafood Provençal at the table. Serve the seafood with potato pancakes and a decorative salad of endive, melon balls, avocado slices, and hazelnuts.

For an impressive company dinner that looks complicated but is not, present the seafood Provençal in the individual parchment packets in which it cooks. Kitchen parchment, sold at speciality food shops and kitchen supply stores, preserves the natural moisture and nutrient content of foods and also cuts down on clean-up time. As the packets heat up, some steam escapes through the porous paper, thereby preventing the food from becoming soggy. Serve the packets unopened so the food stays hot; then, snip them open at the table to release a mouth-watering burst of aroma.

What to drink

Serve this seafood dinner with a delicate and fruity wine Riesling from the Pacific Northwest or Alsace. Or, for a slightly sweeter taste, choose a Riesling from one of Germany's Rhine districts.

Start-to-Finish Steps

The morning of serving

1 Wash lemon and dry with paper towel. Grate enough lemon rind to measure 1 teaspoon for seafood recipe. Halve lemon and squeeze enough juice to measure 2 tablespoons for pancakes recipe and 4 teaspoons for seafood recipe. Halve lime and squeeze enough juice to measure $2^{1}/_{2}$ tablespoons for salad recipe.
2 Follow seafood recipe steps 1 through 9.

Up to six hours before serving

1 Follow pancakes recipe steps 1 through 7.

Thirty minutes before serving

1 Follow seafood recipe step 10 and salad recipe step 1.
2 Follow seafood recipe step 11.
3 While seafood is baking, follow salad recipe steps 2 through 7.
4 Follow pancakes recipe step 8 and salad recipe steps 8 and 9.
5 Follow seafood recipe step 12, pancakes recipe step 9, and serve with salad.

Seafood Provençal in Parchment

Small onion
Medium-size clove garlic
2 medium-size tomatoes (about 500 g (1 lb) total weight)
Small courgette
Small bunch basil
Small bunch parsley
125 g (4 oz) small fresh mushrooms
2 tablespoons unsalted butter
Salt
Freshly ground white pepper
$1/4$ teaspoon dried thyme
1 bay leaf
1 teaspoon grated lemon rind
12 large shrimp
4 fillets of sole (about 750 g (1$1/2$ lb) total weight)
4 teaspoons lemon juice
125 g (4 oz) bay scallops

1   Bring 2 ltrs (3 pts) water to a boil in large saucepan over high heat.
2   Meanwhile, cut 4 pieces of parchment paper into heart shapes about 30 cm (12 inches) deep and 30 cm (12 inches) wide at top. Set aside.
3   Peel and chop onion. Peel and mince garlic. Wash tomatoes, courgette, and fresh herbs, and dry with paper towels. Cut courgette crosswise into thin slices. Mince enough basil and parsley to measure 15 g ($1/2$ oz) each; set aside.
4   Wipe mushrooms clean with damp paper towel and slice thinly.
5   Fill large bowl with ice water. Drop tomatoes into boiling water and blanch 30 seconds. With slotted spoon, transfer tomatoes briefly to bowl of ice water. Drain tomatoes and peel; halve crosswise and squeeze out seeds. Cut tomatoes into chunks.
6   Melt butter in large skillet over medium heat. Add onion and garlic and cook 2 minutes, or until onion is tender. Stir in tomatoes, courgette, basil, parsley, mushrooms, $1/4$ teaspoon salt, $1/8$ teaspoon white pepper, thyme, bay leaf, and lemon rind. Bring to a boil and simmer gently, stirring occasionally, 10 minutes, or until sauce is thickened.
7   Meanwhile, pinch legs off shrimp, several at a time, then bend back and snap off sharp, beaklike pieces of shell just above tail. Leaving tail intact, remove shell and discard. Using sharp paring knife, make shallow incision along back of each shrimp, exposing digestive vein. Extract vein and discard.

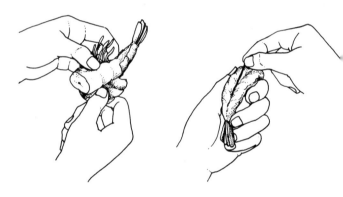

8 Wipe sole fillets with damp paper towels. Place 1 fillet to one side of centre on each parchment-paper heart, tucking under thin ends of fillets. Sprinkle each fillet with 1 teaspoon lemon juice and season with salt and pepper. Place 3 shrimp and one fourth of scallops on and around each fillet. Remove and discard bay leaf from sauce and top seafood with equal portions of sauce.

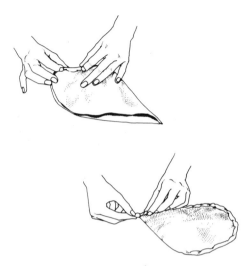

9 Fold parchment paper over filling, bringing halves of heart together. Seal packages by starting at 'V' in heart and rolling and crimping edges together tightly. Twist tip of heart to seal. Place packets on baking sheet and refrigerate until 30 minutes before serving.

10 Thirty minutes before serving, preheat oven to 220°C (425°F or Mark 7).

11 Bake packets 25 minutes.

12 To serve, place a packet on each of 4 dinner plates.

Lacy Potato Pancakes

3 medium-size scallions
500 g (1 lb) Russet potatoes
2 tablespoons lemon juice
30 g (1 oz) plain flour
2 eggs
1/2 teaspoon salt
1/8 teaspoon freshly ground black pepper
3 tablespoons unsalted butter, approximately
3 tablespoons vegetable oil, approximately

1 Wash scallions and dry with paper towel. Thinly slice enough scallions to measure 30 g (1 oz); set aside.

2 Peel potatoes. In food processor, or with grater, shred enough potatoes to measure about 350 g (12 oz). Place in medium-size non-aluminium bowl. Add lemon juice and enough water to cover; stir well.

3 Turn potatoes into colander and drain well. Turn out potatoes onto paper towels and thoroughly pat dry.

4 Combine scallions, flour, eggs, salt, and pepper in large bowl. Stir in potatoes.

5 In large shallow skillet or on griddle, heat 1 tablespoon butter and 1 tablespoon oil over medium heat until hot. Add potato mixture in small amounts, spreading mixture to make thin pancakes (small holes will form). Do not crowd. Cook pancakes 3 to 4 minutes, turning once.

6 Using slotted spatula, transfer pancakes to baking sheet in single layer. Repeat procedure with remaining potato mixture, stirring well before measuring out each portion. Add additional butter and oil as needed.

7 Allow pancakes to cool, cover with plastic wrap, and let stand at room temperature until 10 minutes before serving. Do not let potatoes sit out for more than 6 hours.

8 To serve, heat pancakes in 220°C (425°F or Mark 7) oven 8 to 10 minutes, or until golden brown and crisp.

9 Divide pancakes among 4 dinner plates.

Honeydew-Avocado Salad

Large shallot
30 g (1 oz) hazelnuts or walnuts
Small avocado
4 tablespoons vegetable oil
2 tablespoons hazelnut or walnut oil
2¹/₂ tablespoons lime juice
1 teaspoon Dijon mustard
¹/₈ teaspoon salt
¹/₈ teaspoon freshly ground black pepper
Small head lettuce
Medium-size head Belgian endive
Small honeydew melon

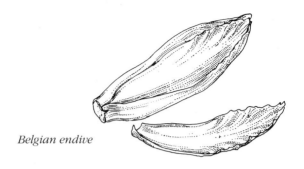

Belgian endive

1 Peel and mince shallot; set aside.
2 If using hazelnuts, place on baking sheet and toast in 220°C (425°F or Mark 7) oven, stirring occasionally, 5 to 7 minutes, or until skins split.
3 Meanwhile, halve and pit avocado. Peel halves and cut into 1 cm (¹/₂ inch) slices.
4 Combine shallots, oils, lime juice, mustard, salt, and pepper in small non-aluminium bowl and whisk to blend. Add avocado slices and turn to coat with dressing. Set aside.
5 Remove hazelnuts from oven and set aside to cool.
6 Wash lettuce; discard any bruised or discoloured leaves. Trim endive and separate leaves. Dry lettuce and endive in salad spinner or with paper towels; set aside.
7 Halve and seed honeydew. Using melon baller, cut enough fruit into balls to measure about 350 g (12 oz). Reserve remaining melon for another use.
8 Place hazelnuts in kitchen towel and rub between hands to remove skins. Coarsely chop hazelnuts or walnuts.
9 Line 4 salad plates with lettuce. Arrange endive, avocado, and melon balls decoratively on lettuce. Stir dressing and drizzle over salads. Sprinkle with nuts and serve.

<table>
<tr><td>

</td><td>

Raclette Casseroles
Marinated Vegetable Salad
Fruit in Filo Bundles

</td></tr>
</table>

Raclette (from the French verb racler, 'to scrape') is best if you use authentic Swiss raclette cheese, which has a firm texture and a mild nutty taste. If it is unavailable, substitute another mild, easy-melting cheese such as Swiss, Jarlsberg, or Gruyère.

The fruit-filled filo bundles are perfect for make-ahead meals because they can be prepared up to 24 hours in advance and held in the refrigerator until you are ready to bake them. Vary the fruit filling according to the season; for example, you can use fresh peaches instead of the pears and apples.

What to drink

A full-bodied white California Chardonnay or good French Chablis would be an excellent selection here.

Start-to-Finish Steps

The morning of serving

1 Wash lemon. Grate enough rind to measure 1 teaspoon each for salad and filo bundles recipes. Halve lemon; squeeze enough juice to measure 1 tablespoon for salad recipe.

Piping hot raclette *casseroles, a vegetable salad with sugar snap peas, and fruit-filled filo for dessert make an elegant supper.*

2 Follow filo bundles recipe steps 1 through 7.
3 Follow salad recipe steps 1 through 9.
4 Follow raclette recipe steps 1 through 7.

Thirty minutes before serving
1 Follow raclette recipe steps 8 through 12.
2 Follow salad recipe steps 10 and 11.
3 Follow raclette recipe step 13, filo bundles recipe step 8, and serve raclette casseroles with salad.
4 Follow filo bundles recipe step 9 and serve for dessert.

Raclette Casseroles

750 g (1^1/$_2$ lb) small new red potatoes
350 g (12 oz) Black Forest ham, in one piece
Salt
Small bunch broccoli (about 500 g (1 lb))
250 g (8 oz) raclette cheese
2 tablespoons unsalted butter
2 tablespoons plain flour
300 ml (10 fl oz) milk
^{1}/$_8$ teaspoon freshly ground black pepper
Pinch of nutmeg

1 Bring 2^1/$_2$ ltrs (4 pts) water to a boil in large saucepan over high heat.
2 Meanwhile, scrub and dry potatoes and cut into 1 cm (^{1}/$_2$ inch) thick slices. Cut ham into 2^1/$_2$ cm (1 inch) cubes; set aside.
3 Add ^{1}/$_2$ teaspoon salt and potatoes to boiling water. Boil, stirring occasionally, 8 minutes.
4 Meanwhile, wash and dry broccoli. Cut broccoli tops into florets. Reserve stems for another use.
5 When potatoes have cooked 8 minutes, add broccoli, reduce heat to medium-low, and simmer 5 minutes, or until potatoes and broccoli are tender.
6 Turn vegetables into colander to drain and cool.
7 When cooled, place potatoes, broccoli, and ham in plastic bag. Close bag tightly and refrigerate until 30 minutes before serving.
8 Thirty minutes before serving, preheat oven to 200°C (400°F or Mark 6). Grease 4 individual heatproof casseroles.
9 Cut enough cheese into 2^1/$_2$ cm (1 inch) cubes to measure 2 cups. Cut remaining cheese into thin strips and set aside.
10 Melt butter over medium heat in small saucepan. Stir in flour, then gradually add milk. Stirring constantly, cook 1 minute, or until smooth. Add ^{1}/$_4$ teaspoon salt, pepper, and nutmeg and continue to cook over medium heat, stirring occasionally, 3 to 4 minutes, or until mixture comes just to a boil. Remove from heat and stir in cheese cubes.
11 Divide half of potatoes, broccoli, and ham among individual casseroles. Spoon 60 ml (2 fl oz) sauce into each casserole and top with remaining vegetables and ham. Spoon remaining sauce over top.
12 Bake raclettes 15 minutes.
13 Top raclettes with reserved cheese strips and bake another 5 minutes, or until bubbling.

Marinated Vegetable Salad

250 g (8 oz) sugar snap peas or green beans
6 radishes
Small red onion
2 eggs
125 g (4 oz) fresh mushrooms
1 tablespoon lemon juice
1 teaspoon grated lemon rind
1 teaspoon Dijon mustard
$1/2$ teaspoon salt
$1/8$ teaspoon freshly ground black pepper
125 ml (4 fl oz) vegetable oil
Small head lettuce

1　Wash, dry, and trim peas or beans and radishes. If using beans, cut into $7^1/2$ cm (3 inch) lengths. Thinly slice radishes. Peel and thinly slice onion. Place radishes and onion in large non-aluminium bowl.
2　Separate eggs, placing yolks in small bowl and reserving whites for another use.
3　Bring $2^1/2$ cm (1 inch) water to a boil in medium-size saucepan fitted with vegetable steamer.
4　Meanwhile, wipe mushrooms clean with damp paper towel and cut into 5 mm ($1/4$ inch) slices. Add to bowl with radishes and onion.
5　Place peas or beans in steamer, cover pan, and steam 3 minutes.
6　Meanwhile, in food processor or blender, combine egg yolks, lemon juice, lemon rind, mustard, salt, and pepper. Process 10 seconds, or until combined. With machine running, add oil in a slow, steady stream.
7　Transfer peas or beans to colander, refresh under cold running water, and allow to drain.
8　Add peas or beans to large bowl.

9　Drizzle dressing over vegetables, toss to combine, cover, and refrigerate until just before serving.
10　To serve, wash lettuce and dry with paper towels. Discard any bruised or discoloured leaves. Line salad bowl with lettuce leaves.
11　Gently toss marinated vegetables and add to salad bowl.

Fruit in Filo Bundles

175 g (6 oz) unsalted butter
2 large pears (about 500 g (1 lb) total weight)
Large Granny Smith apple
125 g (4 oz) plus 2 teaspoons sugar
30 g (1 oz) dark raisins
2 tablespoons plain flour
1 teaspoon grated lemon rind
$3/4$ teaspoon cinnamon
$1/8$ teaspoon nutmeg
16 sheets filo, thawed

1　Lightly grease baking sheet. Melt butter in small saucepan over medium-low heat.
2　Peel pears and apple. Core fruit and cut into wedges, then cut crosswise into very thin slices.
3　Combine 125 g (4 oz) sugar, raisins, flour, lemon rind, $1/2$ teaspoon cinnamon, and nutmeg in medium-size bowl.
4　Add fruit and toss to coat well.
5　Place filo sheets on a damp towel covered with plastic wrap and cover top sheet with plastic wrap and a second damp towel. To make one bundle, lay 1 sheet flat on work surface and brush lightly with melted butter. Top with second sheet and brush lightly with butter. Repeat procedure with

third sheet. Fold fourth sheet in half and centre on stack. Brush lightly with butter and spoon one fourth of fruit filling onto centre of folded sheet.

6 Fold over long sides of filo to cover fruit. Fold over short sides, twisting edges in centre to close bundle. Brush with butter and transfer to prepared baking sheet. Make 3 more bundles in same manner.

7 Combine remaining 2 teaspoons sugar and $^1/_4$ teaspoon cinnamon in small bowl. Sprinkle over bundles, cover pan, and refrigerate until 30 minutes before serving.

8 To bake, place bundles in 200°C (400°F or Mark 6) oven for 25 minutes, or until golden brown.

9 Using wire metal spatula, transfer filo bundles to napkin-lined platter, and serve hot.

Added touch

These ultra-crisp breadsticks made with pumpernickel rye flour can be topped with coarse salt or caraway seeds before baking. Or try fennel or anise seeds.

Pumpernickel Breadsticks

150 g (5 oz) plain flour, approximately
125 g (4 oz) pumpernickel rye flour, or regular rye flour
1 packet 7$^1/_2$ g ($^1/_4$ oz) fast-acting yeast
1 tablespoon brown sugar
1 tablespoon unsweetened cocoa powder
1 teaspoon salt
4 tablespoons vegetable oil
1 tablespoon molasses
30 g (1 oz) cornmeal
1 egg white
Coarse salt or caraway seeds

1 In food processor fitted with dough blade, combine flours, yeast, sugar, cocoa, and salt. Process 10 seconds, or until combined. With machine running, gradually add 60 ml (2 fl oz) hot tap water. Or, combine ingredients in large bowl and stir with wooden spoon.

2 Combine 125 ml (4 fl oz) cold water, oil, and molasses in small bowl. With processor running, gradually add mixture and process until dough forms a ball. Or, add molasses mixture to large bowl and stir with wooden spoon. (Dough will be quite sticky. If it is too sticky to handle, add 1 tablespoon flour. If it is too dry, add 1 teaspoon water.)

3 Process or stir 1 minute more to knead dough. Let dough rest 20 minutes. Meanwhile, sprinkle two large baking sheets with cornmeal.

4 Transfer dough to lightly floured surface. Halve dough and cut each half into 16 pieces. Roll each piece into a 17$^1/_2$ cm (7 inch) stick. Arrange sticks 2$^1/_2$ cm (1 inch) apart on baking sheets. Cover sheets with kitchen towels and let rise in warm place 30 minutes.

5 Preheat oven to 180°C (350°F or Mark 4).

6 Lightly beat egg white with 1 teaspoon water in small bowl. Brush breadsticks with egg white and sprinkle with coarse salt or caraway seeds. Bake 30 minutes, or until crisp. Transfer to rack to cool.

Gloria Zimmerman

Menu 1
(*left*)
Thai Seafood Soup
Ginger Chicken
White Rice

When Gloria Zimmerman was learning to cook Thai and Vietnamese dishes, she needed a teacher to explain the ingredients to her and a translator to help her order them in the ethnic markets, where no one spoke English. Today, to her delight, many more sources offer the exotic ingredients required by these two cuisines. Here she presents two Thai menus and one from Vietnam, all featuring intriguing combinations of colours and flavours – and all suited for make-ahead meals. Although Gloria Zimmerman suggests alternatives for those ingredients that may be hard to get, she strongly recommends using ethnic products to achieve authentic results.

In Menu 1, she prepares a Thai seafood soup called *po taek*. This rich combination of shrimp, fish, mussels, and squid is flavoured with lemon grass and other Thai seasonings and is followed by a main course of chicken cooked with ginger.

A Vietnamese meal, Menu 2 begins with a salad of pork, whole shrimp, and egg strips served over bean sprouts and marinated onions. Although the salad might seem like a meal in itself, in Vietnam it is typically followed by a meat course. Here the cook offers poached chicken bathed in a spicy ginger-garlic sauce.

In Menu 3, the steak for the Thai sour beef salad is broiled early on the day of serving, then, just before dinnertime, sliced and flavoured with fish sauce, lime juice, and hot red or green chili peppers if desired. Sweetened pork slices and broccoli with oyster sauce provide interesting flavour contrasts to the beef. You can also serve rice with this meal.

The Thai seafood soup is a beautiful mix of tastes and textures. As additional seasonings, offer lime juice, fish sauce, and red pepper flakes on the side. Present the ginger chicken and rice after the soup.

Thai Seafood Soup
Ginger Chicken
White Rice

The seafood soup contains a number of ingredients used frequently in Thai cooking, among them lemon grass, dried *galangal* (also known as *kha*), and dried keffir lime leaves (*makrut*). Lemon grass is a tall woody grass resembling a large scallion, with an intriguing sour taste. Sometimes available fresh, but more often dried, lemon grass is sold in Asian groceries. If you buy fresh, use only the portion of the stalk up the point where the grey-green leaves begin to branch off. If you use dried lemon grass, wrap it in cheesecloth for cooking and discard it before serving. An acceptable substitute is the rind from half a lemon.

Galangal (or *galingale*) is a rhizome, like ginger, but with a more delicate taste. Dried *galangal* is inexpensive and can be bought at Thai groceries. If it is unavailable, substitute a 1 cm ($^1/_2$ inch) piece of ginger. The lime leaves come from the keffir lime tree. Most Oriental markets sell the leaves dried; Thai groceries often stock them frozen. As an alternative, you can use fresh lemon or lime leaves or the rind from half a lime.

The chicken dish gains an interesting texture with the addition of tree ear (also known as cloud ear) mushrooms. Sold dried, these fairly bland mushrooms expand to five or six times their original size when soaked. If they are unavailable, omit them from the recipe.

What to drink

Dark, full-bodied beer, served ice cold, is the best beverage for these spicy dishes. Try a Japanese or Mexican brand.

Start-to-Finish Steps

The day before or morning of serving
1   Follow chicken recipe step 1 and soup recipe steps 1 through 3.
2   Follow chicken recipe steps 2 through 5.
3   Follow soup recipe steps 4 through 7.

Thirty minutes before serving 1   Follow soup recipe step 8 and rice recipe steps 1 and 2.
2   While rice is cooking, follow soup recipe steps 9 through 12 and serve as first course.
3   Follow chicken recipe step 6, rice recipe step 3, and serve.

Thai Seafood Soup

2 stalks fresh or dried lemon grass, cut into 5 cm (2 inch) sections, or rind of $^1/_2$ lemon
500 g (1 lb) can straw mushrooms
6 slices dried galangal, or 1 cm ($^1/_2$ inch) piece fresh ginger, peeled and thinly sliced
5 dried keffir lime leaves, or rind of $^1/_2$ lime
500 g (1 lb) mussels, or 250 g (8 oz) crabmeat
250 g (8 oz) medium-size shrimp
250 g (8 oz) squid, cleaned
350 g (12 oz) haddock, sole, or flounder fillets, preferably with skin
3 large limes
175 ml (6 fl oz) Thai fish sauce (nam pla) or soy sauce
Red pepper flakes (optional)

1   Bring $1^1/_2$ ltrs ($2^1/_2$ pts) water to a boil in large saucepan over high heat.
2   Meanwhile, wrap dried lemon grass, if using, in piece of cheesecloth and tie securely with kitchen string. Drain mushrooms in colander.
3   Add lemon grass or lemon rind, straw mushrooms, galangal or sliced ginger, and lime leaves or lime rind to boiling water. Boil 5 minutes, or until stock becomes aromatic. Remove pan from heat and, when stock has cooled cover and refrigerate until 30 minutes before serving.
4   Scrub mussels, if using, and remove hairlike beards. Rinse mussels and place in large bowl. Cover, and refrigerate until 30 minutes before serving.
5   Peel and devein shrimp, leaving tails intact. Place shrimp in medium-size bowl, cover, and refrigerate until 30 minutes before serving.
6   Separate squid tentacles from body sac. Cut body sac open lengthwise and lay flat, fleshier side up: Without cutting through flesh completely, score diagonally in both directions. If squid is large, halve lengthwise. Wrap in plastic and refrigerate until 30 minutes before serving.
7   Wipe fish fillets with damp paper towels. Cut fillets into 5 x $2^1/_2$ cm (2 x 1 inch) pieces. Wrap in plastic and refrigerate until 30 minutes before serving.
8   Thirty minutes before serving, bring stock to a simmer over medium heat.
9   Add squid and return soup to a simmer. Add mussels or crabmeat and return soup to a simmer.

Add pieces of fish and return soup to a simmer.

10 Skim froth from soup. Cover pan and simmer 2 minutes, or until seafood is completely cooked. Discard any unopened mussels. Meanwhile, halve and juice limes.

11 Add 3 tablespoons fish sauce or soy sauce and 4 tablespoons lime juice to soup and stir. Place remaining fish sauce, remaining lime juice, and red pepper flakes if using in small bows to serve as condiments.

12 Ladle soup into large serving bowl or tureen or into 4 individual soup bowls and serve with condiments.

Ginger Chicken

2 tablespoons dried tree ear mushrooms (optional)
500 g (1 lb) boneless, skinless chicken breasts
Medium-size clove garlic
5 cm (2 inch) piece fresh ginger
2 tablespoons vegetable oil
2 teaspoons sugar
2 tablespoons dark soy sauce

1 If using mushrooms, place in small bowl, add hot water to cover, and let soak 20 minutes.

2 Cut chicken into 2^1/$_2$ cm (1 inch) pieces. Peel and mince garlic. Peel ginger and cut lengthwise into thin strips.

3 Drain mushrooms in strainer; discard liquid. Rinse mushrooms well and pat dry with paper towels.

4 Heat oil in wok or large heavy-gauge skillet over medium heat until hot. Add garlic and stir-fry 30 seconds, or until golden brown. Add chicken and stir-fry 3 minutes, or until flesh is opaque.

5 Add ginger and stir-fry 1 minute. Add mushrooms, if using, and stir well. Stir in sugar and soy sauce and remove wok or skillet from heat. When cooled, cover pan with foil and refrigerate until just before serving.

6 To serve, reheat chicken over medium heat, stirring often, 3 to 4 minutes, or until hot. Transfer to platter.

White Rice

^{1}/$_4$ teaspoon salt
300 g (10 oz) long-grain white rice

1 Bring 750 ml (1^1/$_2$ pts) water and salt to a boil in medium-size saucepan over high heat.

2 Stir in rice, cover pan, and reduce heat to medium-low. Simmer gently 18 to 20 minutes, or until rice is tender and water is completely absorbed.

3 Fluff rice with fork and transfer to serving dish.

The dressing for the salad is a classic Vietnamese sauce called *nuoc cham*. It is made with *nuoc nam*, an aromatic fish-based condiment that is as basic to Vietnamese cooking as salt is to Western cuisines. *Nuoc nam* and the similar Thai fish sauce *nam pla* (an acceptable substitute) are sold bottled in Oriental groceries. The word *nhi* on the Vietnamese product indicates that it is of highest quality.

What to drink

Beer or ale suits this menu well. If you prefer wine, a simple dry white, well chilled, would be your best bet. Try a Soave or a Spanish white Rioja.

Start-to-Finish Steps

The day before or morning of serving

1   Halve lime and squeeze enough juice to measure 2 tablespoons for ginger sauce recipe and 1 tablespoon for salad recipe.
2   Follow chicken recipe step 1 and salad recipe steps 1 through 3.

A Vietnamese tiered salad of bean sprouts, onion, pork, shrimp, and strips of egg piques the appetite for chicken in a spicy sauce.

3 Follow chicken recipe step 2.
4 While chicken is poaching, follow salad recipe steps 4 through 10 and ginger sauce recipe steps 1 and 2.
5 Follow chicken recipe steps 3 and 4 and salad recipe steps 11 through 13.
6 Follow chicken recipe step 5 and salad recipe step 14.

Thirty minutes before serving
1 Follow salad recipe step 15 and chicken recipe steps 6 through 11.
2 While rice and chicken are cooking, follow salad recipe steps 16 through 18 and serve as first course.
3 Follow chicken recipe step 12 and serve.

Vietnamese Salad

175 g (6 oz) boneless pork loin roast
125 g (4 oz) medium-size shrimp
500 g (1 lb) bean sprouts
1¹/₂ teaspoons salt
Medium-size onion
100 g (3 oz) sugar
4 tablespoons Vietnamese fish sauce (nuoc nam) or dark soy sauce
1 egg
2 teaspoons vegetable oil
1 medium-size clove garlic
¹/₄ teaspoon red pepper flakes
1 tablespoon lime juice
125 ml (4 fl oz) plus 3 tablespoons distilled white vinegar
¹/₄ teaspoon freshly ground black pepper
Small bunch coriander
2 tablespoons dry-roasted peanuts for garnish (optional)

1 Place pork in small saucepan with 750 ml (1¹/₂ pts) water and bring to a boil over medium-high heat. Reduce heat to medium, cover pan, and simmer 20 minutes.
2 Meanwhile, bring 1¹/₂ ltrs (3 pts) water to a boil in large stockpot over high heat.
3 Pinch off legs of shrimp, several at a time, then bend back and snap off sharp, beaklike pieces of shell just above tail. Remove shell, except for tail, and discard. Using sharp paring knife, make shallow incision along back of each shrimp, exposing digestive vein. Extract vein and discard. Set shrimp aside.
4 Add bean sprouts to boiling water in large stockpot and return to a boil. Immediately turn bean sprouts into colander and refresh under cold water. Set aside to drain.
5 Bring 250 ml (8 fl oz) water and ¹/₂ teaspoon salt to a simmer in small saucepan over medium heat.
6 Meanwhile, peel and thinly slice onion.
7 Add shrimp to simmering water and cook 3 minutes.
8 Transfer drained bean sprouts to large bowl, cover, and refrigerate until 30 minutes before serving.
9 Turn shrimp into colander and set aside to drain.
10 Meanwhile, cut pork into 5 mm (¹/₄ inch) slices; cut slices lengthwise into thin strips. Wrap in plastic and refrigerate until 30 minutes before serving.
11 For dressing (nuoc cham), combine 60 g (2 oz) sugar, fish sauce, and 175 ml (6 fl oz) water in small non-aluminium saucepan and bring to a boil over medium-high heat. Remove pan from heat and set aside to cool.
12 Meanwhile, for shredded egg, beat egg lightly in small bowl. Heat oil in 20 cm (8 inch) skillet over medium heat until hot. Pour in egg, tilting pan to coat bottom thinly and evenly. Cook 20 to 30 seconds, or just until egg sets on bottom; turn and

cook another few seconds. With metal spatula, remove egg from pan; roll up Swiss roll style and cut crosswise into thin shreds. Wrap shredded egg in plastic and refrigerate until 30 minutes before serving.

13 Peel garlic and mince enough to measure $^1/_2$ teaspoon. Place in mortar and pound to a paste with pestle. Add garlic, red pepper flakes, lime juice, and 3 tablespoons vinegar to dressing. Cover pan and refrigerate until 30 minutes before serving.

14 In small non-aluminium bowl, combine remaining vinegar, salt, sugar, and black pepper. Add sliced onion, cover bowl, and refrigerate until 30 minutes before serving.

15 Thirty minutes before serving, set out all refrigerated ingredients to come to room temperature.

16 Wash and dry coriander. Set aside 3 sprigs for garnish and finely chop enough remaining coriander to measure 3 tablespoons. Coarsely chop peanuts, if using; set aside.

17 Spread bean sprouts on serving platter. Top with marinated onion slices and let stand 2 minutes.

18 Carefully drain off marinade from platter and arrange pork and shrimp over onion. Top with shredded egg and sprinkle salad with chopped coriander, peanuts if desired, and 6 tablespoons dressing. Garnish salad with coriander sprigs and serve remaining dressing separately.

Poached Chicken with Rice and Ginger Sauce

1$^1/_2$ Kg (3 lb) chicken, quartered
300 g (10 oz) long-grain white rice
2 medium-size cloves garlic
2$^1/_2$ cm (1 inch) piece fresh ginger
$^3/_4$ teaspoon salt, approximately
Pinch of sugar
Small bunch mint for garnish
Small carrot for garnish
Small cucumber for garnish
1$^1/_2$ teaspoons vegetable oil
Ginger Sauce (see following recipe)

1 Bring 3 ltrs (6 pts) water to a boil in large stockpot over high heat.

2 Add chicken to boiling water, reduce heat to medium, and partially cover pot. Poach chicken 30 minutes, turning chicken pieces once during cooking time.

3 Place rice in large bowl and rinse thoroughly in cold water, rubbing rice between hands. Drain rice and repeat procedure. Turn rice into strainer and set aside to drain.

4 Remove stockpot from heat. Transfer chicken and stock to large bowl, cover, and refrigerate until 20 minutes before serving.

5 Place strainer with rice in large bowl, cover with plastic wrap, and refrigerate until 30 minutes before serving.

6 Thirty minutes before serving, remove rice, chicken, and stock from refrigerator. Peel garlic and mince enough to measure 1$^3/_4$ teaspoons. Place in mortar and pound to a paste with pestle; remove from mortar and set aside. Peel and mince ginger. Place ginger and $^1/_8$ teaspoon salt in mortar and pound with pestle.

7 Sprinkle rice with $^1/_2$ teaspoon salt, sugar, 1$^1/_2$ teaspoons pounded garlic, and 1 tablespoon ginger-salt mixture. Stir to combine well.

8 Wash mint, carrot, and cucumber. Set aside 12 mint leaves for garnish. Peel and trim carrot and grate enough carrot to measure 60 g (2 oz). Dice enough unpeeled cucumber to measure 30 g (1 oz). Set aside.

9 Heat oil in large saucepan over medium heat until hot. Add remaining garlic and cook until sizzling. Add rice and cook 2 minutes, stirring constantly to coat with oil.

10 Measure 425 ml (14 fl oz) chicken stock and add to rice; bring to a boil. Reduce heat to medium-low, cover pan, and simmer 20 minutes, or until liquid is absorbed and rice is tender.

11 Meanwhile, place chicken and remaining stock in stockpot and reheat over medium heat 15 to 20 minutes, or until hot.

12 Spread rice on serving platter. Remove chicken from stock and arrange on top of rice. Drizzle chicken with some ginger sauce and garnish with mint, carrot, and cucumber. Serve remaining sauce separately.

Ginger Sauce

1 medium-size clove garlic
2½ cm (1 inch) piece fresh ginger
3 tablespoons sugar
½ teaspoon red pepper flakes
2 tablespoons lime juice
2 tablespoons Vietnamese fish sauce (nuoc nam) or dark soy sauce

1 Peel and mince garlic. Peel and mince ginger. Place garlic, ginger, and sugar in mortar and pound with pestle to a coarse paste. Transfer to small non-aluminium bowl and add red pepper, lime juice, fish sauce, and 350 ml (12 fl oz) water.

2 Cover bowl and refrigerate until 30 minutes before serving.

Added touch

For this typical Vietnamese dessert, select firm, just-ripe bananas, which hold their shape when deep fried.

Fried Bananas

3 medium-size bananas
125 g (4 oz) plain flour
1 tablespoon baking powder
60 g (2 oz) potato starch or cornstarch
825 ml (1¾ pts) vegetable oil
1 tablespoon confectioners' sugar

1 Peel bananas and cut crosswise into 5 cm (2 inch) long pieces.

2 Combine flour, baking powder, and potato starch or cornstarch in large bowl. Add 4 tablespoons oil and 350 ml (12 fl oz) water and whisk until combined.

3 Heat remaining oil in wok or large saucepan until a deep-fat thermometer registers 180°C (350°F). Dip bananas into batter, place gently in oil, and fry 2 minutes, turning once, or until lightly browned. Using slotted spoon, transfer bananas to paper-towel-lined platter to drain briefly.

4 To serve, place bananas on platter and dust with confectioners' sugar.

Sour Beef Salad
Sweet Pork
Broccoli with Oyster Sauce

For a taste of Thailand, prepare this meal of sour beef salad, morsels of sweet pork, and stir-fried broccoli with oyster sauce.

A primary flavouring ingredient for the sweet pork dish is tamarind water, made from the pods of the Asian tamarind tree and used as we would use lemon juice. You will find cellophane packages containing tamarind pulp and seeds, or jars of concentrated pulp, in Oriental markets. Unopened jars of pulp keep indefinitely.

The oyster sauce that flavours the broccoli is a typical Chinese condiment also used in Thai cooking. It is made from dried oysters, which are pounded and combined with soy sauce and other seasonings and then fermented. You don't have to like oysters to find the sauce appealing, since its flavour tends to enhance, not overwhelm, that of the food. Look for relatively thin oyster sauce that is light brown in colour; thick, dark brown sauce is not of high quality. Once opened, the sauce should be stored in the refrigerator, where it will keep indefinitely. There is no substitute.

What to drink
Cold beer (especially a Chinese brand) or ale should be your first choice here. For wine, consider a dry German Riesling of the *Kabinett* class.

Start-to-Finish Steps

The morning of serving
1   Follow beef salad recipe steps 1 through 4.
2   Follow pork recipe steps 1 through 5.
3   Follow broccoli recipe steps 1 through 3.
4   Follow beef salad recipe step 5, pork recipe step 6, and broccoli recipe step 4.

Thirty minutes before serving
1   Follow beef salad recipe steps 6 through 9.
2   Follow pork recipe step 7.
3   While pork is heating, follow broccoli recipe step 5.
4   Follow pork recipe step 8 and serve with broccoli and beef salad.

1   Preheat grill.
2   Halve 1 lime and squeeze enough juice to measure 3 tablespoons. Reserve remaining lime for garnish.
3   Place steak on rack in grill pan and grill 10 cm (4 inches) from heat 3 minutes. Meanwhile, combine lime juice, fish sauce, and sugar in small non-aluminium bowl. Cover bowl and refrigerate sauce until needed.
4   Turn steak and cook another 2 to 3 minutes (meat should be rare). Transfer steak and juices to platter and set aside to cool.
5   When cool, cover platter and refrigerate steak until 30 minutes before serving.
6   Thirty minutes before serving, set out steak and sauce to come to room temperature.
7   Meanwhile, peel onion and cut into thin rings. Wash lettuce and mint, and chilies if using, and dry with paper towels. Separate lettuce leaves, discarding any bruised or discoloured leaves. Reserve 16 mint leaves for garnish. If using chilies, halve, seed, and cut crosswise into thin slices. Wash remaining lime and dry with paper towels. Cut lime into thick slices. Notch and twist each slice, if desired.
8   Transfer steak to work surface. Cut lengthwise into 5 cm (2 inch) slices, then cut slices across the grain into 5 mm (1/4 inch) pieces. Return steak to platter with juices. If, when ready to serve, juices are still coagulated, place the platter with the steak and juices in a warm oven for a minute or two, then proceed.
9   Arrange lettuce leaves on 4 dinner plates and top with equal portions of steak, juices, and onion rings. Top each portion with 4 mint leaves, and chili slices if using. Drizzle with sauce and garnish with lime slices.

Sour Beef Salad

2 large limes
850 g (1³/₄ lb) boneless sirloin steak, cut 1 inch thick
2¹/₂ cm (1 inch) Thai fish sauce (nam pla) or dark soy sauce
1 teaspoon sugar
Large yellow onion
Small head lettuce
Small bunch mint
4 small fresh hot red or green chilies (optional)

Sweet Pork

1 teaspoon tamarind pulp, or $^1/_2$ teaspoon tamarind concentrate, or small lime
350 g (12 oz) boneless pork loin roast
Medium-size yellow onion
2 tablespoons vegetable oil
$^1/_4$ teaspoon freshly ground black pepper
3 tablespoons dark soy sauce
2 tablespoons sugar

1 To prepare tamarind water, combine tamarind pulp, if using, with 2 tablespoons water in small non-aluminium bowl. Strain mixture and set aside enough to measure 1 tablespoon. Or, dissolve tamarind concentrate in 1 tablespoon hot water in small bowl. Or, halve lime and squeeze enough juice to measure 1 tablespoon; set aside.
2 Cut pork into 5 cm x 5 mm (2 x $^1/_4$ inch) slices.
3 Peel onion; halve onion through stem end and slice thinly.
4 Heat oil in wok or large skillet over high heat until hot. Reduce heat to medium and, stirring constantly, add pork and pepper. Continue to stir-fry 3 minutes, or until pork is no longer pink.
5 Add onion and stir-fry another minute. Add soy sauce and cook 3 to 4 minutes, or until liquid is absorbed. Add sugar and tamarind water or lime juice and stir to coat pork. Remove pan from heat and set aside to allow mixture to cool.
6 When cooled, transfer mixture to medium-size bowl, cover, and refrigerate until about 10 minutes before serving.
7 To serve, reheat pork in large saucepan over medium-low heat until hot.
8 Divide pork among 4 dinner plates.

Broccoli with Oyster Sauce

Large bunch broccoli (about 750 g (1$^1/_2$ lb))
Medium-size clove garlic
2 tablespoons vegetable oil
3 tablespoons oyster sauce
Pinch of sugar

1 Bring 2 ltrs (3 pts) water to a boil in 6 ltrs (8 pts) saucepan over high heat.
2 Meanwhile, wash broccoli and dry with paper towels. Cut tops of broccoli into small florets. Trim and discard woody stem ends, and cut stems on diagonal into 5 mm ($^1/_4$ inch) slices.
3 Add broccoli to boiling water and cook 3 minutes. Turn broccoli into colander and refresh under cold running water. Set aside to drain.
4 Transfer broccoli to large bowl, cover, and set aside at room temperature until needed.
5 Ten minutes before serving, heat wok or large skillet over high heat until hot. Meanwhile, peel and mince garlic. Reduce heat to medium, add oil and garlic, and cook garlic a few seconds, or until golden brown. Add broccoli and stir to coat with oil. Stir in oyster sauce and sugar. Cook 3 to 5 minutes, or just until broccoli is hot. Divide broccoli among 4 dinner plates.

Meet the Cooks

Jenifer Harvey Lang

Food writer and professional cook Jenifer Harvey Lang, a graduate of the Culinary Institute of America, was the first woman to cook at the "21" Club in New York City. She writes for magazines and is the author of *Tastings*.

Marilyn Hansen

Marilyn Hansen, who studied cookery, has worked as food editor of *Family Weekly*. She is currently a food and beverage writer and consultant and is a member of Les Dames d'Escoffier.

Margaret Fraser

Home economist Margaret Fraser lives in Toronto, Canada, where she manages her own consulting business, specializing in food styling for magazines, television and product packaging.

Roberta Rall

Roberta Rall works as a freelance food stylist and home economist. She prepares and styles food for photography for numerous publications; develops recipes for specific food products and audiences; and organizes taste tests.

Gloria Zimmerman

A noted authority on Chinese, Southeast Asian, and French cuisines, Gloria Zimmerman is co-author of *The Classic Cuisine of Vietnam* and was a consulting editor for *The Encyclopedia of Chinese Cooking* and *The Encyclopedia of Asian Cooking*. Besides running her own cookery school, she also conducts gastronomic tours to the provinces of France.

A Wealth of Herbs

Increasingly, herbs are arriving in the markets fresh; the proliferation of health stores and other specialist shops has widened choice, and many cooks with gardens have taken to raising their own. Recent ethnic influences have called attention to once seemingly esoteric herbs. Coriander, for one, is at last gaining deserved popularity in Europe, although cooks in Asia and the Middle East have been using it for centuries.

Anyone wishing to dry fresh herbs can tie them loosely in a bundle and hang them upside down in a cool, dark, well-ventilated place for several weeks. When the leaves are completely dried, strip them from the stems and store them in an airtight container.

Two swifter methods of preserving herbs make use of the microwave oven and the freezer. To microwave herbs, place five or six sprigs at a time between paper towels and microwave them on high for 1 to 3 minutes until the leaves are brittle. Store the leaves loosely in airtight jars.

To freeze herbs, rinse the sprigs and pat them dry. Strip the leaves off the stems and put them into a heavy-duty plastic bag. Gently flatten the bag to force out the air, seal the bag tightly, and place it in your freezer. Use the leaves as the need arises.

Basil (also called sweet basil): This fragrant herb, w its underlying flavour of anise and hint of clove, gc particularly well with tomato.

Chervil: The small, lacy leaves of this herb have a ta akin to parsley with a touch of anise. It is good in s ads and salad dressings. Chervil is popular in Fran where it is often an ingredient in herb mixtures, inclu ing *fines herbes*. When used in cooking, chervil shou be added at the end, lest its subtle flavour be lost.

Chives: The smallest of the onions, chives grow in gra clumps. When finely cut, the hollow leaves contrib their delicate, oniony flavour to fresh salads and r vegetables. Chives should always be used fresh, as dri ones are virtually tasteless.

Coriander (also called cilantro): The serrated leaves the coriander plant impart a distinctive fragrance and flavour that is both mildly sweet and bitter. Coriand leaves should be used fresh or added at the end cooking if their flavour is to be appreciated fully.

Dill: A sprightly herb with feathery leaves, dill enhanc cucumber and many other fresh vegetables, as well fish and shellfish. When used in cooking, dill should added towards the end of the process to preserve delicate flavour. Both dill seeds and dill leaves can